1960

THE FOUR LAST THINGS

THE MACMILLAN COMPANY
NEW YORK · CHICAGO
DALLAS · ATLANTA · SAN FRANCISCO
LONDON · MANILA

IN CANADA
BRETT-MACMILLAN LTD.
GALT, ONTARIO

THE
FOUR LAST THINGS

Collected Poems

by

SISTER M. MADELEVA, C.S.C.

New York
THE MACMILLAN COMPANY
1959

Nihil obstat   Daniel V. Flynn, J.C.D.
                     CENSOR LIBRORUM

Imprimatur   ✠ Francis Cardinal Spellman
                 ARCHBISHOP OF NEW YORK

July 27, 1959

First Printing

The Macmillan Company, New York
Brett-Macmillan Ltd., Galt, Ontario

Printed in the United States of America

Library of Congress catalog card number: 59-13782

To My Favorite Author

Dear God,
Herewith a book do I inscribe and send
To You Who are both its beginning and its end;
A volume odd,
Bound in some brief, allotted years,
Written with love and tears;
Fragments of which You are the perfect whole
Book of my soul.
Break, break the sealing clod
And read me, God!

Preface

The verse in this volume was written, pretty much in the order assembled, sectionwise, over the past forty-five years. The Christmas poems were gathered from the half-dozen small volumes four years ago to make a gift book, *American Twelfth Night*. No revisions have been made in the verses themselves except a change from the solemn to the simple form—*you* for *thou* and *thee*—in three or four instances.

This second and more complete edition of my collected poems may very well stand as a record of my experience in verse writing during my life as a Sister of the Holy Cross. In the history of literature this is not of the slightest importance. But for many young writers it may provide help and even encouragement.

We all work under the great American pressures: so much work; so little time. We are all waging our own particular battles with words, making every word fight for its life in a line or a paragraph. We all experience the elation of our first insight or inspiration, then the struggle with its body of words, our nausea of disgust and finally the joy of achieved expression.

Because of the number of young persons who write to me for direction I say these things. The processes of creative writing are as secret and comparably as holy as gestation. The parallel is close. Nothing can be so fatal to work—perhaps I should limit this to a poem—as to discuss it before you have it under your own control, before it is yours beyond dissolution or theft. Saint John Baptist de La Salle used to warn, "A good work divulged before its time is half destroyed."

This book that you have in hand is as good as I can make it and as copious in terms of my limitations of ability and time. These I have used, however, with utter frugality. I have never had leisure for writing, save such times as one takes to recover from flu, winter colds, fatigue, if these can be counted leisure. I have never written a poem that I have not sold to some good magazine, or published in book form before it had time to go through the periodical waiting line. My words have had to work for their living.

This, too, I submit to young writers as a counsel of economy. Poetry is a distillation, not a diffusion; a high concentrate, not an atomizer. It is hard work. It can be the fruit of the Sixth Beatitude.

But if you have written poetry you know or are learning all these things. If you have not and will never even try, well—is it too late to skip this preface?

SISTER M. MADELEVA, C.S.C.

Contents

KNIGHTS ERRANT

PENELOPE

AMERICAN TWELFTH NIGHT

KNIGHTS ERRANT

Knights Errant

Death is no foeman, we were born together;
He dwells between the places of my breath,
Night vigil at my heart he keeps and whether
I sleep or no, he never slumbereth.
Though I do fear thee, Knight of the Sable Feather,
Thou wilt not slay me, Death!

But one rides forth, accoutered all in wonder;
I know thee, Life, God's errant that thou art,
Who comest to make of me celestial plunder;
To wound me with thy Love's immortal smart!
Life, thou wilt rend this flesh and soul asunder;
Love, thou wilt break my heart!

Surrender

If you are merely conscious clay,—ah! well,
Tire not such stuff with futile, tread-mill climb,
Which lifts to leave you level with the slime;
Nor think that death can break your earth-born spell;
Clay has no heel Achillean, vulnerable.
Be animate till some deliberate time
Shall choke and crunch you to potential grime,
For you are fit for neither heaven nor hell.

But He Who made you cousin to the clod
First plunged you in the Spirit Which is He
Whence you have risen, divinely armed and shod
To scale the ramparts of eternity.
Already stricken with the shafts of God,
You fall a prisoner to Deity.

A Song for a Man

You, man, have a home and a wife and a child; what song do you sing?
I have a mate on her nest with a little blue egg under each gray wing,
And for joy of this thing
I sing,
Sing to my brooding bird-wife of the skies above her,
Sing of the birdlings now soon to awake 'neath the soft breast of her,
Sing at the dawn, at the dusk that I love her, I love her!
A bird on a nest with a little blue egg under each gray wing
Is a simple thing;
For the heart of a woman, the soul of a child, O man, what rapturous song
    do you sing?

The Mendicant

Mendicant Day, how are you clothed and fed!
In the gray robe of morning garmented;
Upon your tireless feet time's eager shoon,
Your simple fare, the white crust of the moon;
And for your thirst, into dawn's shining cup
The lark's clear song is poured for you to sup.

No scrip nor purse have you, intrepid one,
To hold your alms, the pale coin of the sun.
The house that welcomes you, there will you bide.
The troubled world his door may open wide.
Enter, unworthy though it be, and say,
"Peace, peace be to this house," good Brother Day!

You Sang in My Dream

You sang to me, dear, last night through all of my dreaming,—
O, why did you sing?—
To know that your song and my joy are only seeming
Is a bitter thing.

For into your voice all our multiplied loves came thronging,—
Dreams have heartless ways,—
And then I awoke to this numb, inarticulate longing
Of silent days.

Of Dust

I said to my body, "Be mindful thou art an offender,
Thou art dust of the dust, thou art slime, thou art clod of the clod."
But my body made answer, "O soul, I am blind with the splendor
Of the promise of God."

"Methinks, O my body, that thou shouldst be compassed with sadness,"
I said, "who hast tasted of life and must yet taste of death";
"But know, I have breathed," said my body, "to ecstatic gladness,
The breath of God's breath.

"And this clay will pass from me, and life, aye, and death, like a vapor;
I shall rise at His word, light as light, quick as thought, swift as wing;
For though dust, soul of mine, even dust in the hands of its Shaper
Is a glorified thing."

In Salem Town

The road from Nazareth to Salem town
Is far to-day;
I do not think a stranger going down
Could find the way.

Time was that every year a holy pair
This glad way trod;
Time was One walked content beside them there,
The young Boy, God.

I wish that down this road to peace again
The Boy would go,
And, meeting Him upon the way, that men
Would see and know.

I wish three endless days in Salem town
The Child would stray,
Till all its priests and doctors of renown
Must find His way.

In the Way

Held eyes and foolish hearts had they
Who walked to Emmaus the day
The dead and deathless Son of God
Beside them as a stranger trod.

Perhaps it was a way with them,
For often in Jerusalem
Their ears had listened to a Word
Nor understood the things they heard.

Their eyes had seen in Galilee
Wonders that prophets longed to see;
Their hearts had stirred to fear and doubt
Things that must make the stones cry out.

Such wonders and such wonderings
Were no uncommon happenings.
Slow hearts, unseeing eyes they had
The while they pondered and were sad.

But know you, this had come to pass,—
Their hearts had smitten been as grass,
And their poor eyes beggared of sight
For looking on unveiled Light.

And they had died of seeing God,
Had He not been in lowness shod.—
I think he walks beside me thus
What times I go to Emmaus.

I Go to School

I seek a teacher and a rule,
Dear Brother Francis, and a school
Where I can learn to be a fool.

The world is erudite to-day;
The folk of Gubbio and your gray
Brother Wolf are dead, they say.
　　Sweet friend of Christ, yourself shall be
　　My book of gentle courtesy.

A single purse, a single cloak
Do scarce suffice for modern folk;
Such foolishness as once you spoke
  About your Lady Poverty,
  That, poverello, tell to me.

Bird songs in Umbria were sweet,
Or else, mayhap, your quaint conceit
Found meanings now quite obsolete.
  God's little one, please share with me
  Your sister birds' sweet psaltery.

Stars nebular and wise, indeed,
Above Averno shared your creed
Of piercèd heart and wounds that bleed.
  Enamored Knight of Calvary,
  Teach me love's madmost ecstasy.

Behold my teacher and my rule;
Yourself, St. Francis, are my school;
God give me grace to be a fool!

Sister Death

Doff your mourning robe, my Sister; I have for you raiment new,
The very stuff of glory, golden and white and blue.
Your darling feet in sorrow no longer shall go shod;
Here are shoon of divine impatience for trafficking with God.
Your hands, my little Sister, are very young and cold;
See, I bring my life's one blossom for their still, white strength to hold.
Such eyes you have are strangers to tears of sorrowing—
Let me grow sick with longing—for they gaze upon the King!
I wait at your quiet doorway, beneath love's architrave;
Unloose its bolts and lead me into the golden grave.
Lovely my Death, constrain me, I would be comforted;
My sweetest Sister, kiss me,—whisper that I am dead.

The Poet's House

For Joyce Kilmer

We built, that day, in our soldier's way
A house of clay for a house of clay,
"A house with nobody in it,"
As he used to say, in his poet's way—
The man who had lived in that house of clay—
Then we paused for a heart's long minute
To grieve and to pray; "In Thy Godlike way
O God, rebuild this house of clay
For Thy lover who dwelt within it,
With a flag and a cross athwart the skies,
A soldier's house in paradise
With the soul of a poet in it!"

For Your Birthday

Dear, I would spread the wide earth for your table,
And light the stars for tapers, every one,
And kindle, at their dying, were I able,
The lordly sun.

And I would set a banquet for your pleasure,
Brave with brave things my soul is dreaming of,
Glad as my heart is glad, above all measure
Sweet with my love.

But through the dawn I see two candles burning
At a white board where you with Christ are fed;
Lo, how your heart is filled and all its yearning
Is comforted!

The Beggar

"I am mistress of my house," said I.
"When that vagrant beggar, Love, comes by
He shall not enter nor ever know
That he breaks my heart, though he come or go;
I will bar the doors lest he be nigh."

Came Love, the lord; all the gates flew wide;
I watched him walk like a king inside
While I sat at the portal begging bread;
I fain had been with a morsel fed,
And, but for the crumbs from His board, had died.

Wind Wraith

A shy ghost of a wind was out
Tiptoeing through the air
At dawn, and though I could not see
Nor hear her anywhere,
I felt her lips just brush my cheek,
Her fingers touch my hair.

Mountain Tops

Mountains and resting clouds and climbing trees,
The higher climbing sun, you show me these.
O, if I saw but mountains and clouds and trees

I think perhaps my heart could bear the thing;
The autumn would not burn me, and the spring—
I might not so much dread the miracle thing!

Young Moon

He comes, a gay and golden star
Climbing the topmost hills of night;
Past where white mountain summits are
He takes his perilous path of light,
Gallant and bright.

A cavalier of plume and curl
Is he, upon his lady's quest;
Look where she goes, exquisite girl,
In whiteness of shy silver dressed,
Walking the west.

The Pepper Tree

On a night the sun and the earth and the weather
And their brother, the wind, all slept together.

And it happened while they were slumbering
That each one dreamed of a different thing,

And then awoke.
The wind first spoke.

"I dreamed," said he,
"Of a fairy tree."

"And I," said the weather,
"Of a fairy's feather."

Spoke the earth, "My dream
Was all agleam

"With rubies red
Of fairies." Said

The sun, "Mine made
A fairy glade
Of delicately woven shade."

Then they laughed, did the sun and the earth and the weather
And the wind, as they put their dreams together.

But I wonder if ever these gay lads knew
That the pepper tree on that same night grew.

A Snow-Capped Mountain in Summer

The white hours of your maidenhood are past;
Your passive morning wakes into life's young noon;
The virgin coronal slips from your brow at last;
Your first love waits, asking yourself for boon.
See where before your motionless feet is cast
The burning and unquenchable heart of June.

White Peace

The whiteness of the moon is on the world,
Sleeping and beautiful;
Across the blue remoteness drifts and clings
The wandering whiteness of a single cloud.
One passionless mountain lifts its face to heaven,
Wrapped in white peace and very far away.
To the quick bosom of the earth is pressed
The fragrant whiteness of a little flower.

The light of your white soul shines on my life,
And in my heart the whiteness of your love
Burns always.

Roses for My King

(The Stigmata of St. Francis)

If that my King should say,
"Fetch me of roses five most fair to-day,"

Where, think you, could I find
Flowers to please His heart, to please His mind?

Straight would I go to him
Who stands forever next the seraphim,
And say, "Here, at his feet,
Are roses, Master, that your heart deems sweet.

"And from his hands there spring
Blossoms that worthy are of You, my King.

"One flower more doth bide
Within the lovely garden of his side.

"See how its petals part,—
O God, it is the blossom of his heart!"

Dear Master, bid me, pray,
Bring You of flowers the five most fair to-day;
Look You, where I will find
Roses to please Your heart, to please Your mind.

Contents

What's in a book?
Something that I have writ,
Illustrious
By all your high soul finds in it;
For thus
My words from your white thoughts grow luminous;—
That's in a book.

A Letter to My Most High Lord

This letter do I write to Thee,
My Lord most high,
To say I love Thee and to make
A quest hereby.

Thou knowest that Thy mother is
My Lady dear;
Thou knowest that I make small songs
For her to hear.

Of late my little singing words
Have fled away,
And she has had no song, sweet Lord,
This many a day.

Wherefore I ask thee, do Thou bid
Some angel bring
Unto my Lady dear the songs
I cannot sing.

O, let it be an angel small
With simple ways
Who will not feel it mean to chant
My childish praise.

This is the quest, my Lover Lord,
With which I come;
And though Thou strike my tongue, my heart
Forever dumb,

I will exchange for sweets of song
One thing more sweet,
The silence of adoring lips
Against Thy feet.

A Young Girl Writeth to Her Father

My Father, I wrote Thee sometime a letter.
Dost remember,—the matter was on a song?
But now I would ask Thee for something better,
A thing I have waited for long and long.

I know full well that upon my pleasure
The veriest thought of Thy heart is bent;
I know that thou givest me without measure
All that can bring to my soul content.

This country, sweet Sire, whither Thou hast sent me
Is passing lovely and fair to see;
It should, in truth, if aught could, content me
Away from home and apart from Thee.

But ever a golden shadow falleth
Whither-so-ever my child heart turns,
And a voice as of many waters calleth,
Calleth—O Sire, how my wild heart burns,

Knowing not why; and then I am lonely,
Lonely where erst I had happy been,
Homesick for Thee and desiring only
To see the face I have never seen.

Now I close with love, hoping Thou wilt borrow
Some little moments to answer me,
Sending me word that upon the morrow
I may come home, Father, home to Thee.

The Theme

Always the selfsame word, day upon day;
The little songs I sing, the prayers I pray,
My boldest thoughts of Thee run all one way:

"I love Thee,"—ever, ever, "I love Thee,"
Until I fear that Thou must wearied be
To have no other speech than this from me.

What sayest Thou, sweet my Lover?—"Do not I
Tire of the tireless sun, the constant sky,
The faithful stars forever slipping by?

"Doth it not vex Me that upon the beach
The tides monotonous run? Will I not teach
The never-changing sea some newer speech?

"Am I not weary that all trees are stirred
By willful, changing winds; that every bird
Hath but a single, albeit a liquid word?

"Nay, should I tire of seasons and the sun,
Till time its last, unfaltering course hath run
Tell Me thou lovest Me, My precious one!

"When, on some ultimate day, in sudden bliss
I catch thee to My heart in death's fierce kiss,
I shall have naught to say to thee but this:

" 'I love thee, love thee!' Wilt thou wearied be
To hear thy poor, one word eternally?"
Nay, changeless One, it is enough for me!

Enough, too, this, that Thou shouldst bid me say,
"I love Thee," till the shadows flee away,
Till light dissolves the darkness, and the day

Breaks, and upon the waiting silence thrills
Thy word forever, and its glory stills
The yearnings of the everlasting hills.

God Hath This Lullaby

(For Lenore)

Come, child of My heart;
All the little, young lambs of My flock have for long been a-sleeping;
And, lamb that thou art,
I take thee, too, tenderly, tenderly into My keeping,
Never from thee to part.
Here all of My bright, singing angels shall mind thee;
And here, when they seek thee, thy father and mother shall find thee
Asleep on My heart.

Rest sweetly, My own;
All the blossoms that grow in My garden are folded in slumber,
White blossom, half blown;
And O, with what golden, glad dreams beyond dream, beyond number
My garden is sown!
Here no rough wind of earth can affright thee or shake thee,
So sleep, lovely flower, till I call thee and kiss thee and wake thee
In heaven, My own.

Travel Song

Know you the journey that I take?
Know you the voyage that I make?
The joy of it one's heart could break.

No jot of time have I to spare,
Nor will to loiter anywhere,
So eager am I to be there.

For that the way is hard and long,
For that gray fears upon it throng,
I set my journey to a song,

And it grows wondrous happy so.
Singing I hurry on for oh!
It is to God, to God, I go.

With Sound of Trumpet

"Oh! a horn is a reckless thing to blow,"
Cried a wild young wind very long ago;
Then with lips to a mountain canyon pressed
He blew a blast from the east to the west.
For that is the way of the wind, you know.

Oh! a horn is a conquering thing to blow.
Seven times around the city go
The silent armies. The trumpets sound;
The breachless walls fall to the ground,
And that is the end of Jericho.

"Oh! a horn is a magical thing to blow,"
Mused a shepherd lad, "or loud or low,
Out of its wakened heart I bring
Peace to my flocks and repose to my king;—
But what of the day when it is not so?"

Oh! a horn is a fickle thing to blow.
Orléans, Rheims,—hear its triumph grow!
But in Rouen's square there is no sound,
Only smoke rising from the ground,—
A piteous way for the Maid to go!

Oh! a horn is a terrible thing to blow.
At its call tremendous of weal or woe
The books shall be opened, the seals unsealed,
The beginning and end of all revealed.
This is the way of God, you know.

Bread and Wine

Seekest an altar, Lord? Take my awaking,
    Alight with tapers kindled in the east,
Decked with the dawn's full bud, to blossom breaking.
    Thy priest, O Lord—and who shall be Thy priest?
    The dawn itself that lifts to Thee my sacrificial feast.

What sacrifice, what feast? Could I but borrow
  The fruit of years that never may be mine!
But all my folded life, my every morrow,
  Change on this morning altar into Thine;
  And let my soul's glad life be bread, my heart's red
    love be wine.

Defense

God grant that heaven's defender grow not mild!
Upon a time he found a guardsman sleeping,
Sheathed sword and idle armor vigil keeping;
"Angel," he spoke, "thy honor is defiled!"
The awakened spirit answered, "See, a child
I keep, who keepeth me; with weeping
The night is sown, he of it joy is reaping."
" 'Tis well," the stern archangel said and smiled.

The world and I have eaten bread of sorrow,
The world and I have drunk to death of sin;
Great Michael, let our guardian spirits borrow
Thy naked sword, O heaven's paladin;
Defend our leaguered gates that on the morrow
The King of hosts may fitly enter in!

Raiment

Immaculate! When thus the Godhead thought,
Mary upon creation's threshold stood;
Mortality her still soul's whiteness caught,
And round the Word, that our redemption brought,
Wrapped the safe garment of her motherhood.

Garment of Flesh and Blood, late bread and wine,
Daily I don this raiment wrought for me.
O Christ, be Thou a wedding robe divine!
Around my soul's poor nakedness let shine
Thy white apparel of divinity.

Bondage

And I, if I lifted up, will draw all things to Me;
Wherefore, O heart! know that thou art not free
Save from sin's malices.
Thou art My captive for eternity.
My cross thy prison-palace is,
The bands of My strong arms encircle thee,
My heart a chalice is;
Thy sentence hear, love's penalty;
Drink of this God-filled cup thy death, thy life to be!

Post-Communion

The feet of Christ are set in human places;
How shall I tell of ways by which they led
Who only know I hungered and was fed;
And presently I came to luminous spaces
Where hands were lifted toward me, eyes, and faces,
And voices pleaded past me, "Thou hast said,
'Come to Me, ye who would be comforted!'"
These things I knew, O Christ, in Thy embraces!

These things I knew and felt, and comprehended
That Thou walkest not with me alone, apart;
Thou comest with a retinue attended
Of sorrows, Man of Sorrow as Thou art;
That I may feel, till time and tears be ended,
The tides of life that break against Thy heart.

The Mystic at Table

Water and bread,
Meager fare spread
Before my body whence my soul is fed.
Water to lave me
Out of that piercèd side open to save me;
Bread which in five I part
To dip in wounded depths of hands and feet and heart.
Water and bread
Transfigured, whence I am divinely fed,
Awe-fully comforted,
Knowing not if I miss,
Or am caught up to this,
Thy breathing bosom, Christ, Thy living kiss.

Candlemas Day

Through what obscure, half-comprehending night
Thou shinest, Christ, for light!
Candle and flame Thou art,
Set in the candelabrum of my heart.

March

Of what tumultuous grief these tears are token!
I wipe them with the wind which is my hair;
And now my alabaster box is broken,
Spilling the breath of lilies everywhere.

Winter, my Lord, let all the seasons tell,
I do these things against thy burial.

In the Hill Country

Men heeded not this thing,—
A young maid into Juda hurrying,—
But when birds waked to sing,
And buds to blossoming,
When every leaf and petal, wind and wing,
Thrilled with articulate joy, "Our King, our King!"
Men said that it was spring.

Grace Notes

The winds are alilt with the year at the spring, the world that is new;
The birds send spilt raptures of song on the wing up to skies that are
    blue;
I stand on the threshold of Maytime and sing, Lady Mary, to you.

Pageantry

A world of gladness fills the way,
And joy proclaims a holiday.
Expectant blossoms throng earth's street
Where grass spreads carpet for the feet
Of spring who passes, clothed in May.

But to my heart such glad array
Is heaven's lovelier pageant-play,
And as its lady passes, sweet,
My soul's shy love awaits to greet
My queen, my mother, clothed in May.

Red Tulips

God wrote it;
I quote it;
All ye, do ye note it
On the margin of spring,
This homely apostil,
This miracle thing
Pentecostal!

"A dozen dull tulips were gathered together
In fear, every one;
When sudden arose a great stirring of weather,
Of wind and of sun,
And there sat on each tulip a parted tongue whether
Of petal or flame!"—lo, their gospel of life has begun!

Assumpta Est Maria

One only Word
I kept for all my speech, by night, by day,
Alway, alway,
Which I upon the lips of God had heard.

And I had thought
This living Word of living love would be
Speech endlessly
When I should be in arms of love upcaught.

Now I am come
Upon, within the arms of my desire,
Nor word require;
My lips against the lips of love are dumb.

A Pied Piper

Brave Piper October, what tune do you blow
That the leaves are bewitched and wherever you go
They flutter and follow, agleam and aglow?
From oak tree and bramble, from high tree and low,
They flock to the sound of the piping they know,
And down from the tall trees of heaven, O ho!
Come dancing and glancing the white leaves of snow.

Autumn

For that I dreamed the night long of my lover
I must be clad today most radiantly.
Come, earth and air and sky;
Put all my outworn summer raiment by.
Gold I will wear
For all my golden dreams of him and fair;
And red,
The burning memory of one beauteous word he said.
Sky, earth, and air,
Think you my love is come, the importunate rover?
Quick, fetch me a mist of purple for my hair,
And for my hand
A single snowflake flower,
Sign of my passing hour.
See how all beautiful I stand
Waiting—ah! who could guess,—waiting for death, my lover.

The King's Highway

Upon the purple splendor of thy way
This simple garment of my song I lay,
My heart's appareling,
Where through the white warp of thy vested days
Thine and thy Father's praise
I weave and sing.
If, as they pass along,
Thy feet but touch this woven path of song,
Changed is it to the highway of a king.

Or, should I silent be,
A myriad clamorous tongues on every tree
Would chant a gold and scarlet rhapsody;
The very stars beyond their farthest fires
Point the celestial truantry of thy desires;
And acquainted heaven hath but one word to tell,
"He hath done all things well."

This is thy purple vintage time, thy golden hour of reaping;
What fruits of fertile days, scattered afar
Upon the fields of life, quickened with weeping,
Upgathered are,
God hath forever with thee in His keeping.

How do I falter!
How doth my tongue
Impotently
Fail both myself and thee,
While all thy multitudinous praise unsung
Prostrates itself at thy predestinate altar.
The wide earth's garnering of wheaten sheaves
And unpressed fruitage of the vine
Thrill at their potencies of bread and wine,
Beneath thy breath quiver like shaken leaves,
Tremble and start.
Lo! it is done;
Thou and thy Christ are one;
These are thy Flesh and Life-blood of thy heart.

Such cloak of song I lay
Before thy heavenward passing feet this day,
Mortal immortal clod,
Impurpurate indeed!
How art thou saturate with God
Whose hands are clasped between strong hands that bleed!

I Bless Thee, Notre Dame

The news I have for heaven will brook no waiting,—
I will mount up my song's immediate stair
And call, importunate, at the cerulean grating,
"I would have speech with Edward Sorin, he is there!"
"Knowest thou where?"

Anticipate angelic question! Straightway
I pause upon my topmost step of song,
All joyously perplexed at the celestial gateway;
My search for one resplendent soul in that great throng
Must needs be long,

And where the tri-crowned soul of Sorin may be
I only dream, and see with touchèd eyes
A virgin host,—but if the spotless Lamb's white way be
His single beatific path I but surmise.
Vision replies,

"Soldier, apostle, priest, triune forever
Before a Triune God in triple bliss
The sainted Sorin stands." Foolish, I cry, "Ah! sever
Thy heavenly restraint, our father, meet and kiss
In soul, thy soul-dream, this—

"This, the consummate hope of the waiting years,
This unfolded flower of consecrate sod,
Quickened with breath of thy love, wet with thy tears,
Soul-petaled blossom of God.

"See,—and say if this be earth's ultimate mystical rose,
This burgeoning beauty of arch and dome and spire,
This multiple Holy of Holies where glows
The Eucharist's multiplied fire;

"This miracle wrought of soul and heart and brain,
Aye, even this Kingdom of God upon earth;
And measure thy life, all the love and the pain
By their ultimate, infinite worth.

"Behold this incorporate thing, more fair than in vision seen.
To this City of God royal pilgrims of cross and crown
Are come, bearing tribute of praise, while thy Queen
In apocalypsed splendor smiles down."

Faileth my song; responsive, clad in wonder
The soul of Sorin glows, deific flame;
His speech is benediction, clothed in Jehovah's thunder,
"By God," his spirit thrills, "and in His holy name
I bless thee, Notre Dame!"

The Quest

Wind of the west, wistful wings, tireless feet,—where are you going,
Hastening, blowing?
When will you rest?
Is there no place you will bide, all your journeying over,
Wanderer, rover,
Wind of the west?

Mountains,—what thoughts in your heart lie a-sleeping, wishful and
    tender,
Wrapped in cloud splendor?
What is your dream?
River,—say, whose are your singing and all of your joy? say, what shall
    come after
Such dreams and such laughter,
Mountain and stream?

Deliberate stars that wide-eyed through the blue night go silvery walking,
Of what are you talking?
Tell me your quest;
Say to me where is the place of your brightest regard, your most beautiful
    shining,
Past my divining,
Stars of the west.

"Oh!" says the wind, "blow with me to the pleasant, green isle of my
    questing,
Eager, unresting;
So—it is near";
"Go," say the mountains, "where rises the bold brow of Slieve Gallon
    yonder;
Him do we ponder,
Distant and dear."

"Low on my heart," sings the river, "the voice of Moyola is falling,
Calling me, calling;
How can I roam?"
"Come," cry the myriad stars, "we will light you the way back to Derry!"
Ah! who could tarry?
Stars, take me home!

Unto the End

Thy tabernacle Thou hast set within the sun,
And figured in the moon on heaven's coast
The elevated host—
Ah, eager haste of the Eternal One!
With joy anticipate
And power consummate,
Lacking Thy mirrored likeness in mortality
Thyself Thy Priest must be,
Raising in fingers consecrate
Thy orbèd Sacrament but mystically.

Gone are the myriad years of waiting,
To Thy eternal present as a day,
Symbols have passed away;
Thy stolèd priest but knocks at heaven's blue grating,
His bidding heard,
Cometh the Word
Incorporate in Bread and throbbing Cup,
That all the world may sup;
Thy Spirit's hunger-thirst is stilled and stirred
Above the banquet which Thy priest holds up.

This is Thy Son beloved, Thou art well pleased,
Filled is Thy promise—infinite suspense—
In glad omnipotence
Thy everlasting longing is appeased.
Lest Thou again shouldst thirst
Or hunger, lo, I durst
Thy life-breath breathe with lips abashed and pale;
In blessèd fingers frail
And finite, rests the Infinite Who first
Raised to Thy lips this Bread, this Holy Grail.

How long wilt Thou, O God, in time's swift fleeting
Suffer that I the Body of my Lord
With sacrificial sword
Thus slay, sweet Lamb of God, daily repeating
His and my Calvary?
Thy Spirit rests on me,
I am Thy priest forever; time's alarms
Threaten but futile harms;
Lifting the pure, white Body of Thy Christ to Thee
Myself am lifted safe to Thy dear arms.

PENELOPE

Penelope

Penelope never has raveled as I have raveled;
She never has fashioned the fabrics that I have spun;
And neither her heart nor her lover has traveled as mine has traveled
Under the sun.

Her web of delay, deliberate, passionate, splendid,
Was tense with allurement, I doubt not; was wet with tears;
But love found it raveled, unfinished—a burial robe—and ended
Those piteous years.

My fingers run wildly through warps of bewildering wonder,
Or dream over woof of caught silence or sudden song;
They tighten on patterns of laughter or fear that is stricken thunder!—
O Love, how long?

Is it naught that I pause in my web as yon suitor woos me;
That I ravel at night with regret the design of day;
That loneliness sickens, grief dazes, and doubt pursues me
With You away?

With a lifetime of years do I lash myself to You and bind You,
Do I dare all the seas of the world without compass or star;
Past the lands of Calypso and Circe and Scylla I seek You and find You,
Be it never so far!

So I fare on the deific pathway my Love has traveled
As I fashion the web that Penelope could not have spun,
And ravel the heavenly robe of delay that she could not have raveled
Under the sun.

If You Would Hold Me

It is so very strange that, loving me,
You should ensnare the freedom I find sweet,
Catch in your cunning will my flying feet.
I will not barter love for liberty;
You cannot break and tame me utterly,

For when your careful conquest is complete
Shall victory be swallowed in defeat.
You hold me only when you set me free.

Because my straight, wild ways are in your power
Do not believe that I surrender them.
Untrammeled love is all I have to give.
If you would keep it, do not pluck the flower;
Leave it, I beg, unbroken on its stem,
Wild with the wind and weather. Let it live!

Patrins

Yes, I shall leave these patrins as I go:
Plucked grasses here, a few blown blossoms there,
To tell you, though I've gone, how much I care;
To tell you, also, should you want to know,
The way I've taken, my beloved, so
That you can find me, find me anywhere.
Be still, my heart! You know he does not dare
To follow dreams; have you no signs to show?

Only the wide, white comfort of the stars,
And strange, lone rest within the arms of dawn,
And love that binds, and truth that sets me free.
Why should you fear such infinite prison bars?
The wild and wistful way that I have gone
Leads but to peace. Belovèd, follow me.

On This Condition

Oh, do I love you? Yes, to be brief and plain.
But from my window, if the day is clear,
See that far mountain, lonely and austere,
Flush into gradual wonder, where has lain
Passionless, pallid snow. Almost like pain
Rose-splendid radiance wraps it in beauty sheer
As the sun kisses it—wait, wait, my dear—
And passing, leaves it virgin white again.

When we have reached those heights of calm surrender
Where white integrity and love are one,
Then you may compass me with utter splendor,
Nor shall we need to wish our joy undone;
Then you may kiss me, love, or tense or tender;
Then you may shine on me, being my sun.

The Black Knight

Will naught but sorrow's dregs your heart appease?
You told or read me that last time you came,
Out of a poem you'd written; even its name
I have forgotten; only you asked the lees
Of life for comfort, bitterer than the seas.
I taste with terror all the innocent shame
You dare; its torture burns me like a flame.
Will nothing satisfy your love but these?

I did not tell you that I found you brave,
Nor bid you wear my colors on your crest.
What secret vigil made you sorrow's slave,
And bound ecstatic anguish to your breast,
What ultimate siege of bitterness you crave
You did not tell me, but I should have guessed.

Tribute

I have known mountains when the day was new
Clothed beyond beauty's self in morning splendor;
Have seen them stand like queens, serene and tender,
Against noon's high tranquillity of blue.
I have watched purple mists and rose-white dew
Cling to them, and the young moon, frail and slender,
Shed on them silver homage of surrender.
I have known this of mountains—and of you.

You are the majesty of all my days,
Set in an aureole of morning light,
Set in my life's high noon; against its night
You will be yet the beauty of my ways.
Ah, let me be the moon, crescent and white,
Shining before you, mute with love and praise!

Ultimates

Although you know, you cannot end my quest,
Nor ever, ever compass my desire;
That were to burn me with divinest fire;
That were to fill me with divinest rest,
To lift me, living, to God's living breast.
I should not dare this thing, nor you aspire
To it, who no less passionately require
Love ultimate, possessor and possessed.

You who are everything and are not this,
Be but its dream, its utter, sweet surmise
Which waking makes the more intensely true
With every exquisite, wistful part of you;
My own, the depths of your untroubled eyes,
Your quiet hands, and your most quiet kiss.

Marginalium

I think the story of Shalott is wrong;
Oh! not the "four gray walls and four gray towers,"
The placid isle and prettiness of flowers,
Nor the sweet incongruity of song.
The river slipping by the summer long,
The lads and lasses, barley fields and bowers,
The listless maid, weaving the livelong hours,
The knight; all these are proper; these belong.

But not youth cursed by love, unwitting how,
Drifting to death upon a senseless tide!
Girl, let your mirror break, your web blow wide;
Nail love's bright flag with life's upon your prow.
Know that you have not ever lived till now.
Who said that love would curse and kill you, lied.

Futility

I have to dress you in your shroud
(A crude device, by no means new)
And look on you who are so proud
To worms consigned, to ashes bowed,
To keep my heart from loving you.

I have to call your faults by roll
(Who once had sought to find them few)
To scrutinize your flaws of soul,
Then memorize and cite the whole
To keep myself from wanting you.

And when I painfully have taught
My mind to scorn you and forget,
I look upon the thing I've wrought
So futilely. It comes to naught.
I love you and I want you yet.

To One Procrustes

"He thinks too much: such men are dangerous."

Do not misunderstand the smile
I send from my Procrustean bed;
It means that in a little while
It shall have done and I be dead.

The bed's dimensions are precise;
One simply must be made to fit;
The methods it employs are nice,
Exact, and there's the end of it.

Once I was stretched to fit its length—
I bear about me yet the scars—
Until I grew to dangerous strength
And was much taller than the stars.

Now, I had grown a head too tall—
The selfsame thing may happen you—
So I am being trimmed, that's all;
It was the obvious thing to do.

The process goes on, day by day,
And I shall never question why;
But when my head is cut away
I think that I may hope to die.

The King's Secret

I

PSYCHE SPEAKS

The King's secret is a great secret, and she is so little to share it,
Sweet sister, my Body, so timid and fragile to bear it;
For she has a lover—the child!—to think of it only
At first will affright her; will leave her all wistful and lovely and lonely.

I shall speak of it to her quite simply, in this wise—O, heavenly duty!—
"Little sister, a King comes to seek you, desiring your beauty.
With the kiss of His mouth He will kiss you; His right arm will enfold
    you;
With His left He will pillow your head, little bride; on His heart He will
    hold you.

"He will ravish you utterly with the white rapture of endless caresses
Till all that you are and possess He inhabits, possesses.
Ah! look in my eyes;—do you know; do you fear to discover
Who He is that comes seeking your beauty, this King Who is God and
    your Lover?"

II

INVITATION

So come, Fair;
At the portal of her house Your little love is waiting;

Though somewhere
In her shy, strange heart she fears You, hesitating.

O come now!
For that she is wild she wishes You to woo her;

Though somehow,
For she is a child, she would that You pursue her.

Still come, Sweet;
Into Your arms' wide peace, passionate and tender,

Will come, fleet,
Brave, Your little love, in exquisite surrender.

III

THE BODY SOLILOQUIZES

Who speaks of bridal bed and nuptial splendor
Waiting the royal Bridegroom and His spouse?
These cannot match the innocent couch I tender
The King Who comes to rest within my house.

O blessed nothingness, whence I am able
To furnish forth my Love this little room;
A little bed, a little chair, a table,
A candle's halo in the shining gloom.

There should be flowers where the King reposes,
With subtle fragrance to beguile His rest;
I place, for bridal lilies, bridal roses,
My white, unfolded self upon His breast.

IV

SURGE, AMICE

Winter is in Your heart, You say, and birds have flown
And flowers are withering;
Sweet, may a shy girl bring
To You, her Love, her garden's only own
Darlings from lands where it is always spring?

Three flowers I pluck for You:
This red rose of my lips, warm with the south;
See how it trembles and rests
Upon the hungry kiss of Your uplifted mouth
Against whose drouth
I press,
In mute abandonment beyond caress,
These other two
Pale, passionate, beautiful blossoms of my breasts.

Now is my garden ravaged utterly;
Let be!
Winter is over and gone; a few birds sing
Within Your heart—and in my arms is spring.

V

AS ONE FINDING PEACE

The secret of the King possesses me
Unutterably.
I am a child to sudden woman grown
Who never yet has known
Invasion so imperious, so complete,
Blindly and madly sweet.
I am a bud to sudden blossom blown,
Intoxicate, replete
With fragrance most divinely not its own.
I am dew thirstily drunk up
Out of dawn's lifted cup.
I am my own impotent, daring self, plunged in a sea
Ecstatically!

O God, encompass me!
Be infinitely mine to hold, to bound me;
Absorb, consume, encompass and confound me;
Be in me and beneath me and above me;
O Father, love me, love me!
Tremendously be,
Strong God, my sea.

In ultimate joy upon this Lover's breast
I come to rest.
Peace, like a song,
Envelopes me;
Peace, like the night,
Folds me in conscious, beautiful delight.
Never has human love held me in tranquil thrall,
For not to human love does peace belong.
What if I be for the Lord God a wall,
Beauteous as cedar and as cedar strong;
What if I be a door, and sealed to all save Him,
Cunningly joined, guarded by flashing cherubim?
I am a door, a wall, a tower of passionate strength
Around which multitudinously throng
Wild ecstasies, wild loves, unending blisses,
A God's caresses and a Father's kisses.

Presently let this rapture in profounder rapture cease;
A silver bulwark of wrought silence be,
My Father, since that I am come at length,
Captive and free,
Into Your presence as one finding peace.

The Swimmer

Afraid? Of you, strong proxy lover, you, God's sea?
I give you my small self ecstatically,
To be caught, held, or buffeted; to rest
Heart to your heart, and breast to breathing breast;
To know on arms and cheeks, on brow and lips the bliss,
The stinging madness of one infinite kiss;
Daring your most exquisite, sweet alarms
In the safe compass of the everlasting arms.

To the Initiate

My kiss upon your brow,
Subtle and cool and continent,
Is two parts vow
And two parts sacrament.

But to your lips I press
Only the white flame of desire;
If two parts are caress,
Two parts are cleansing fire.

Because you understand
This word beyond life's weak replies,
Belovèd, take my hand;
Belovèd, close your eyes.

Apocalypse

My honest mirror shows me wistful eyes
That look beyond me, calm, inscrutable, wise,
Into transcendencies I do not know,
Down ways illuminous that I can not go.

My lips are strange to me; they seem to wear
A quick aloofness from some other where,
As if they wait or cherish some caress
Too secret and divine for me to guess.

I look with quiet wonder at my hands
As one who knows, yet scarcely understands
That they are mine, yet only lent to me,
Waiting some sweet and beautiful destiny.

My ears—I have not caught the hidden word,
Sudden, ineffable, that they have heard;
Nor known how surely and divinely far
My feet have walked on paths familiar.

It is the yearning of my heart they share,
The burning rapture of my soul they dare,
Love's first apocalypse; and rapt and dumb,
They wait the Lover's voice, "I come, I come!"

Your Name

I was half fearful lest the envious night,
Coming upon my slumber stealthily,
Should guess the secret of my still delight
And take Your name from me.

Wherefore I would not trust my lips to keep
That word ineffable, that word of love,
But folded it upon my heart to sleep,
Clasping my hands above.

Deliberate, lovely morning found me thus,
Nor sought to leave one shining splendor there,
Only Your name, than sun more glorious,
Than moon and stars more fair.

And then I do not know which sooner came;
Waking, or my hands gently pressed apart,
And on my lips the sweetness for Your Name
Uprising from my heart.

It seems almost too beautiful to say,—
I had distrusted night and dreaded dawn,
For O, to seek You at the break of day
And find You gone!—

But day has now no wonder matching mine,
Nor subtle night in marvelous silver shod,
Because my heart has held a word divine,
Has kept the name of God.

Concerning Certain Matters of Dress

I

QUESTIONS ON A NUN'S HABIT

You do not think it is because I do not share
A woman's subtle weakness for the piquancy of dress,
Its swift, sure coquetry, its studied carelessness,
That I wear what I wear?
You do not think it is because I do not dare
Its recklessness?
What do you say
Of wearing one's bridal gown
To town
To church on Good Friday?
Of wearing one's shroud
Every day, all day,
In the heat and in the crowd,
On Easter and Christmas day?
You do not tell me that I have bad taste,
Or none at all, or that I am less than fastidious and proud.
Is it because you do not wish to waste
Words upon one whose world in secret you deplore?
You are not sorry for me.
You do not think me dressed quite unbecomingly?
(You would give much to be attired so adequately?)
Of all the dozen gowns I ever wore
And have abandoned, orchid and shadow-gray and powder-blue,
This is the only one that you need envy me.
—You have not ever cared to find me beautiful before,
Have you?

II

OF CROWNS

For captious fashion and capricious fad
I have but small concern or little care.
Not even to plait a belt for Galahad
Should I have shorn the locks that men thought fair;
But for my Lover Lord, divinely glad
I doff the shining crown that was my hair.

III

JEWELRY

Pearls such as yours a proud queen quaffed one day;
A jealous queen such diamonds flung away;
Your ring once Portia might have haggled for;
Your bracelets finer are than Esther wore.

A queen brought me my beads from Nazareth,
Egypt and Judah; she was done to death
Almost in fetching them. What bitterness
She bore, from this cross you, perhaps, can guess.

Her only Son was nailed upon it—see,
Jesus of Nazareth, on Calvary;
And this inscription Pilate fastened there.
Beads are the only jewelry I wear.

Good Out of Nazareth

I

MAYTIME

If Maytime in this golden land
Is sweet as death,
How heavenly fair it must have been
In Nazareth!

If flowers here a glory are,
What had they been
Abloom about the feet of her
Who is their queen!

The little winds that here blow wild,
Grown gentle there,
Adoringly had touched her cheek
And kissed her hair.

And O, if heavens here are blue,
What lovelier skies
Had they beheld, deep mirrored in
Their lady's eyes!

When Maytime here is loveliest
I catch my breath
To think how fair it must have been
In Nazareth.

II

THE JUST MAN

I am with various griefs acquainted well;
Through tense and tender days at Nazareth
I walked with anguish bitterer than death,
And doubt less merciful and kind than hell.
There, too, came utter loneliness to dwell,
(My loved one tarrying with Elizabeth).
I have not piteous word nor piteous breath
The bitterness of Bethlehem to tell.

It is not bitterness will break my heart,
But this; a mother's smile, a Babe's weak cry,
A little cheek to stroke, a hand to kiss!
Ah! I could push the stars of heaven apart,
And dare the awe-full face of God most high
For strength to bear such ecstasy as this!

III

RETURN

O holy house of Nazareth,
Your quiet door,
Open to greet your Lord's return,
Need wait no more.

O mother, leave off listening;
No ear shall tell
Of those returning, wounded feet
You love so well.

He comes, more sudden-sweet than wings
On rapturous quest,
And you are clasped within His arms,
Close to His breast!

The Young Priest's Mother

Yes, he is mine if miracles of weaving
Flesh from my flesh and blood into the fine
Potencies of white manhood, every line
Perfect past mute desire or proud believing
Can make him; if the mystery of achieving
Out of a human son this son divine
Owes aught to motherhood, then he is mine
Beyond my body's gift, my soul's conceiving.

And I am his beyond the extremest guesses
Of men, bound by indissoluble bands
Forever. It is not only he who blesses
And holds me close, but oh! he understands
Why adoration burns in my caresses,
What wounds I kiss upon his beautiful hands.

Proud Boast

Inconstant Peter, what is this you dread,
This word a servant girl speaks scornfully,
"Surely thou wert with Him in Galilee"?
For shame! Whence has your vaunted courage fled;
Where now is your quick sword, unscabbarded.
What boast, O Simon, could more glorious be;
"Thou art of Christ; thy speech betrayeth thee"?
Damsel, this word of yours has been well said.

I charge you, have the selfsame thing to tell
Of me, when in the outer hall of death
I wait the end, inexorable and grim;
Proclaim then to the councilors of hell,
"This man with Jesus was, of Nazareth;
Even his dying speech betrayeth him."

My Windows

These are my two windows; one
Lets in morning and the sun,
Lets in tranquillity and noon,
Lets in all magic and the moon.

One, looking on my garden, shows
Me miracles; a sudden rose,
A poppy's flame, a tulip's cup,
A lily's chalice lifted up.

Wonder-windows! who could guess
The secret of their loveliness?
Beyond transfigured sky and clod
My two windows show me God.

Fantasy

Do you suppose
The cherry tree's white furbelows,
The pretty frills the jonquil shows,
The maple's curious, knotted bows,
The first, pale ruffles of the rose
Are baby things that April sews
For the sweet world to wear?
Who knows?

Desert Sunset

Sunset stood at the edge of the world, apart in the west,
Virginal, calm, aloof, in golden austerity dressed.

Soft little twilight winds and birds and clouds had flown;
Sunset stood on the lone horizon, wistful, alone,

Clad in dispassionate amber from foot to beautiful head,
Whence all the shining, shimmering glamour of life had fled.

Almost I thought her a queen, so splendidly simple she stood;
Almost I thought her a poet in the arms of an elate mood,

Until I saw the day look down at her from the blue
In vain, and the night look up in vain; then I knew

That virginal, consecrate, lone must sunset forever be,
Taking her mystic way to the heart of eternity.

Aye, and my soul stood there, too, at the utter edge of the world,
Plighted, like her, and elate, in golden wonder furled.

Bernadette Takes Leave of Her Flock

Dearlings, my flock, how safe ye be;
How glad ye skip; ye wander free;
Ye sleep so warm and safe. Ah, me!

Shepherdess Mary through the cold
Watched on Bethlehem's wind-swept wold;
One young Lamb was all her fold.

Dearlings, my lambkins, as ye lave
And quench your thirst at the gracious Gave
Some drink for another Lambkin save.

For Shepherdess Mary—she, so mild—
Fled by night through the desert wild,
Fled with her Lamb that was her Child.

Dearlings, my littlest lamb, and all,
Down on your knees in pity fall;
Here is grief that will your dumb hearts appal.

Shepherdess Mary stood beside
The cross where her Lamb was crucified,
Nor did not die when her one Lamb died,

Nor made no moan, nor did not weep!
She is the shepherdess to whose keep
I give you all, my darling sheep.

She will walk the pastures, unseen of you,
In her kirtle white and her girdle blue,
And a golden rose for each small shoe.

So I leave you, dearlings, but safe ye be;
Glad may ye skip and wander free;
Shepherdess Mary folds you for me.

Another Lourdes

No crutches hang before this little shrine;
No chant uprises from a movèd throng;
But who has touched with strength the clinging vine?
Whence has that bird its ecstasy of song?

No votive candle at this grotto glows;
No mystic stream with healing fraught is there;
But who has lit the taper of the rose
Or drunk the living font of children's prayer?

Here is no miracle of hidden might
But who shall speak of bondage and release?
Whence, O my blinded eyes, this sudden light;
Whence, O my waiting heart, this longed-for peace?

Seat of Wisdom

STROPHE: SALUTATION

Others before to-day,
Mary, have hailed you Seat of Wisdom, Grace of the Way;
Others have watched the dawn
Break from that desolate darkness that you trod upon,
As in deific promise first they heard
Spoken that word
Transcendent, that a cursèd world should feel
Salvation, Woman, through your potent heel.

Kings have, in song elate, ecstatic dream,
Had you for theme;
Prophets have sung
In what array your beauteous flags are flung.
In sheer delight
The sun, eclipsed, glories to find you bright;
And for your crown
Precipitate stars have flung their burning splendor down;
The moon beneath your feet
Has set itself for silver pathway, Sweet.
The emulous cherubic hosts might well have striven
For that august evangel unto Gabriel given,
Word consummate
To you, of womankind predestinate.
Beyond all meed desired or dreamed or heard
Elected you God, the Word;
But all the rest might well
Have silence been, desolate more than hell
Save that you said
God's will in you should be accomplishèd.
Hail, Mary, Seat of Wisdom, Grace of the Way!
We greet you as archangels and as children may
And kneel, your plighted daughters, at your feet,
Waiting your answer meet.

ANTISTROPHE: WISDOM SPEAKS

You wait my word.
What answer shall I give more meet than that she heard
Who was to give,
First among women, name to my high prerogative;
My soul doth magnify the Lord, for He

Hath done to me
Things too ineffably beautiful to tell.
For not in Jacob do I dwell;
No, not in Israel nor Salem town
Of high renown.
Ah! come that you may see,
My daughters, where my beauteous dwellings be.
The heavens were not unfurled,
From the beginning and before the world,
Daughters of humankind,
Think that the everlasting God had me in mind.
The poles were not brought forth,
The south's fertility nor the might of the north.
Water was not articulate in any stream or fountain,
Nor earth ambitious was of hill or mountain.
Only with me
Was the sufficient Godhead pleased unutterably.
Eternally within my breast
Wisdom had built her nest,
Until was done
This, that a virgin should conceive and bear a Son.
Content and spaciously has lain within my womb,
The one inn of the world that gave Him room,
Christ; and this chaste and sure retreat
Is Wisdom's holy seat.

EPODE: DEDICATION

What think you of this woman, Mary,
As daily she plies back and forth and up and down
The tasks of home, the errands of the town,
Simple and kind and ordinary

The day long? O, but when night comes to keep
Still vigil, she flies to the arms of God to sleep.
Can this be Wisdom's queen?
Note this to her renown:
She wrought embroidery in the temple, rare;
She dwelt in Nazareth, obscure, serene;
She fashioned swaddling garments for her Child to wear;
She wove the seamless robe that served Him for all save shroud;
She heard Him hailed and jeered at by the crowd;
She saw Him done to death.
What wisdom is there here, what consummate art,
What save the pity of a mother's broken heart?
Her ways were silent ways, but when she spoke
Omnipotence manifest within her Son awoke.
Her ways were prudent ways—
Be that remembered in these later days.
Our path is plain to see;
Ah, let us emulous be
Of her who from eternity has been
Wisdom's sole queen.
Mother, within your halls, beneath each spire and dome,
Welcome us home.

The Bishop Calls

Frederic is at the door to meet him,
With James and John in the hall to greet him;
Mary Lucia, darling thing,
Is on her knees to kiss his ring.

Frederic climbs in the chair beside him;
James and Lucia almost hide him,
Perched at each arm; upon his lap
Sits John enthroned, sweet little chap.

There the four settle themselves sedately
Around the bishop, serene and stately.
The grown-ups gasp in amused dismay;
His Lordship insists that they are to stay.

Perhaps you consider this quite appalling
In children when the bishop is calling,
Because you do not know, I suppose,
The things that a child or a bishop knows.

The Dreamer

I see you, lad, against the painted hill
Lost in such dreams as you are dreaming still.

Your brothers all apparel have more sober
Than yours, October,

Nor boasts in all his glory Solomon
The coat of many colors you have on.

The Game

Dear little girl, thou art playing;
What may thy sweet game be?
A mighty realm thou art swaying,
Lady of high degree,
With royal hosts obeying,
And the Lord Sovereign paying
Thee gentle fealty.
I see;
Dear little girl, thou art praying;
All heaven waits on thee.

To Swing You

You want me to swing you way up high,
Up through the branches, up to the sky,
Higher and higher yet, until
You catch your breath and your heart stands still;

And I watch you, lovely flying thing,
A sweet, bright bird of a child on wing,
With eyes all shining and lips apart!
On a sudden I catch you to my heart.

There, little girl, I can swing you far
Past the topmost branch, past the day-quenched star
To that heaven away beyond the sky;
I can swing you as high as my love is high.

To a Young Girl

Sweet girl, adieu—
Word literally true—
It is to God that I relinquish you.
The gate of your white life, apocalyptic pearl,
Swings quickly to
And you have passed from me into God's keeping.
Already in this first immortal hour
Your young years, which like petals did upcurl
In promise exquisite, unfold, unfurl
To perfect, heaven-blown, and forever fadeless flower,
Your lovely blossomed self. O, child, why am I weeping?
God saw you ripe to sudden fruit, to this swift reaping.
Adieu, sweet girl.

A QUESTION OF LOVERS

A Question of Lovers

There be lovers who bring me roses, the velvet of buds upcurled;
But only one lover gives me the blossoms of all the world.

There be those who have pearls, have rubies; but how can I care for
    these?
This night will my true love bring me the moon and the Pleiades.

I have tokens, if gifts could buy me, till love and its quest be done.
Who will catch me a cloud's white splendor; who will fetch me the dying
    sun?

Or who, on the wings of the morning, will hasten, when dawn is sweet,
To meet and possess me solely? One only, with piercèd feet.

And who, for he loves me truly, will give me as token this,
This poignance of love unspoken, two wounds in his hands to kiss?

Riddles One, Two, and Three

My lover is a fool more wise
Than Solomon;
My lover is a bird that flies
Into the sun.

He is a lighted lamp, my love,
A midnight cry,
A mortal worm that died to prove
He could not die.

My lover is a cedar tree
With branches spread;
A sweet and bitter fruit is he,
Alive and dead.

My lover is a quiet rain
Falling on fleece;
My lover is or endless pain
Or endless peace,

Or sometime an instinctive mole
Breaking the clod;
My lover is a thief who stole
The name of God.

Conceit

If lovers could make summer, could make spring,
What delicate gifts at dawn, at evening
To tremulous sweethearts would all suitors bring!

And think how fine, how loverlike to say,
"Prithee, wilt take my posy, sweet; 'tis May?"
Or, "With my heart I bring thee June today."

Dearer than any light on land or sea
This thing has come to pass. Exquisitely
My love is making April just for me.

I Will Remember Rahab

Rahab was a harlot and lived in Jericho;
Neither was respectable. That was years ago.

She had no scented virtues; she told easy lies;
Her practice was flagrant. Once two spies

Came to her door, their lives at stake;
She took and hid them for the Lord God's sake.

They left her house; they left the town;
The next thing she knew the walls fell down.

She hung a scarlet cord from her window ledge;
It was her sign, it was their pledge.

She heard the trumpets; she heard the shout
Of people in tumult, of city in rout.

The men and the women, the young and the old
Were killed by the sword, so I am told;

But her father and her mother knew no ill
Because of the cord at Rahab's window sill.

I remember Rahab to this day,
And I honor her womanhood for all you say.

It called for mercy and it called for pluck;
You wouldn't think a harlot would have such luck.

It Happened in Sennim

It happened in Sennim that Jabin's host
By the hand of a woman was stricken and lost.

The captain, Sisara, fleeing for life,
Came to the tent of Haber's wife.

He asked for water; she gave him milk
And put him to sleep on a couch of silk;

Then took her cloak to cover him.
The thing that follows is ghastly grim.

She drew a tent nail from its place;
She knelt down close to the captain's face

And drove the long nail through his head.
The soldiers found him that way, dead.

The hosts of Jabin fled away
And Israel was saved that day.

A song was made about the thing
For those who had a heart to sing;

But there was no song in the heart of Jael,
I think, as she drove in the long tent nail.

From the Book of Esther

"Give a fool rope"—the saying goes;
Aman has enough, I suppose.

On his own gibbet, twenty ells high,
He dangles now between earth and sky.

Mardochai rides, by the king's decree,
In silk sky color for the world to see;

And my people, suddenly snatched from death,
Dream not the hazard that bought them breath.

Meanwhile, I in a royal garden
Change my life for their peace and pardon;

Change by the accident of beauty
A girl's young self for a brave queen's duty.

Beauty was all I had to use,
And life was little enough to lose,
And happiness nothing at all to choose.

Jehovah lighted my beauty's flame.
It shall burn for the king in Jehovah's name,
Returning to beauty whence it came.

What matter who reads in this thing that's writ:
"Beauty and youth and a little wit
And a rope with a fool at the end of it!"

Mary of Magdala: Autobiography

Seven expert and competent devils have harassed me all the day!
They have knotted so deftly my hair I can scarce unbind it;
They have hidden my most subtle perfume; I cannot find it.
My lips they have reft of their kisses, my eyes of their tears;
My heart they have stricken with hardness; my soul they have shaken
with fears;
And the end is not yet, possessing what power they do over past, over
possible years.

In the presence of anguished chagrin, in the face of familiar dismay
I have little to say.
I have doggedly faced the sharp issue, exploited, defined it.
Their nice malice I guess and defy once for all! What if now I should
humanly mind it?
They are devils at best who beset, but who never, who never
Can touch my sure peace. I despise them and daunt them forever!
Let them measure efficiency's utmost by every device they may know or
possess or discover.
I have one foolish weapon of love. I have Christ for a lover.

Of Wounds

I have no word to match with its white wonder,
The garment of His body as He wore it
On that first dawning that He came to me
After His death.

Some things there were the soldiers played at dice for,
Kirtle and cloak, perhaps; each got a part
Of such dear raiment as He had about Him,
But not this single garment that He wore.
For that was mine, out of my body woven
Into the pattern of the Son of God,
Seamless from head to foot, and perfect,
Growing to fit His growth, strong with His strength,
Until the day He died.

That day the soldiers tore it, soiled it, spat upon it,
Flayed it to shreds, seared it with gaping rents.
Being His mother, I shall not forget it.

Only for joy I did forget on that first morning
That He returned to me, clad in its splendor
Cut from the loom of death.

Being His mother, I had wished His body flawless,
Fearing to think how beautiful might be
Five open wounds upon it.
I know now that they are as beautiful as God.

The Child

I have a very little game to play;
I have a very little song to sing;
But they are beautiful, and all the day
I cannot think of any other thing.

I take no care of busy passers-by
Nor heed at all the feet that come and go;
I do not even stop to question why
None guess the wonders of this world I know.

My play, though simple, keeps not things the same;
They change, bewilder me, are hard, are new;
But tense with pain or joy, they make my game
Even more beautiful that they are true.

And oh! the childish song upon my lips
May be a happy lilt the whole day long,
May be an anguish from my heart that slips
Its valorous guardian—but is still a song!

I play alone, except for One, always;
And after He has shared my little things,
He catches to His heart the child that plays
And kisses on her lips the child that sings.

I Visit Carmel

Your eyes of infinite kindness meeting mine,
Your hand of quiet resting in my hand
Had been as comforting as oil and wine,
As sweet as water in a desert land.

But in this still room, hopelessly serene,
Why should I seek you, difficult and dear;
In these strange silences with peace between,
How should I vainly think to find you here?

A voice as luminous and cool as dew
Is near me, though I saw not whence it came;
And you are here, sweet, inexplicable you,
Making miraculous music of my name.

Your voice, precursor in my wilderness,
More blessed is, more clear than sight to me;
If there be beauty else I cannot guess,
When you have healed me and when I shall see.

Only I know beatitude begun;
Only I feel no let of cloister bars;
For I have seen a splendor past the sun,
Have heard a voice beyond the listening stars.

Song Silence

Yes, I shall take this quiet house and keep it
With kindled hearth and candle-lighted board,
In singing silence garnish it and sweep it
        For Christ, my Lord.

My heart is filled with little songs to sing Him—
I dream them into words with careful art—
But this I think a better gift to bring Him,
        Nearer His heart.

The foxes have their holes, the wise, the clever;
The birds have each a safe and secret nest;
But He, my lover, walks the world with never
        A place to rest.

I found Him once upon a straw bed lying;
(Once on His mother's heart He laid His head)
He had a bramble pillow for His dying,
        A stone when dead.

I think to leave off singing for this reason,
Taking instead my Lord God's house to keep,
Where He may find a home in every season
        To wake, to sleep.

Do you not think that in this holy sweetness
Of silence shared with God a whole life long
Both He and I shall find divine completeness
        Of perfect song?

I Enter Oxford

It was a bird first spoke to me at Oxford
Through the white fog a single, tentative word.
There were, that daybreak, in my new world only
I and a bird.

I had no grateful syllable to answer,
No littlest sign to say I understood
That lyric word to me, more brave than sunlight,
More kind than food.

Oh! there are bells and there are spires at Oxford,
Ancient, heartbreaking, wordless, splendorous things;
Only to me belongs this simple, silver
Welcome on wings.

Thus Found I Spring at Winchester

Past ancient tower and gate swung wide,
Past ancient arch I walked; inside

Between two doors, close by the wall
Six apple trees stood, young things, all

Unblossomed, delicately still,
Ankle-deep in daffodil.

Two were grave as maids can be;
Two stretched shy, small hands to me;

And two, pretty, wantonwise,
Smiled with April in their eyes.

When I askèd them their name
Sweet as themselves the answer came,

Spoken for no other ear
Save enchanted mine to hear,

Quaintly by each several maid,
"We are cleped Spring," they said.

—And So I Am Betrayed

You spoke of loneliness before I went;
You knew that I would be too proud to show it,
In which security I was content.
You did not say the mocking-bird would know it.

Longing you mentioned in a casual way;
You thought the sea and mountain-trails might bring it;
Knowing, you were too merciful to say
The mocking-bird, the mocking-bird would sing it.

Hunger and thirst and loneliness have come;
This wild, this poignant singing has unmade me;
It is not pride but longing holds me dumb.
The mocking-bird, belovèd, has betrayed me.

The Foolish Sentry

Night and the stars have come to town.
The wind walks up; the wind walks down,
Beneath my window, beside my door.
The wind knows not what the night is for.

He frights off sleep, the comforter;
He fights off sleep, the ravisher;
He lets no ghost of a dream pass by.
What though I wait for sleep, the spy,

To bring me a word of oblivion,
The wind will watch till his watch be done!
Never shall I consort with sleep
While he has the ward of my gate to keep.

Sentry, why do you stalk my door?
Waking is not what the night is for.
Fool, let my gate unguarded be
That sleep, the blessed, may come to me.

Protest Imperative

Just what would it profit us, were I the oak, you, being the wind,
Would buffet me, torture and shatter me, helpless to bend me to mood of
  your mind.
Or were I the pine tree, subduing to music your vagrant unrest,
You, windwise, would slip the wide noose of my arms, the intricate snare
  of my breast.

And let us not speak of the grass, prostrate to be trampled by you,
Scarce lifting its head as you pass to look after the feet it can never
  pursue.
Leave off being the wind! I, your lover, have no taste for these:
The prostrate abjection of grass; the futile, the impotent power of trees.

March Quatrains

I

A herald bluebird on the hawthorn tree
Sits listless, too irresolute to sing;
He waits—none more precocious-grave than he—
Oh, not his mate, but dillydally spring.

II

That meadow lark—the fellow knows his charm—
Need only sing, and I can not resist him;
He does my prosaic self much innocent harm;
But—hear him now!—no, I would not have missed him.

III

The gray oak-brush saves for a bonnier day
Its tasselled green, too frugal-wise to don it,
Counting one lyric blossom brave display,
That pert, capricious towhee swaying on it.

In Desert Places

God has a way of making flowers grow.
He is both daring and direct about it.
If you know half the flowers that I know,
You do not doubt it.

He chooses some gray rock, austere and high,
For garden-plot, trafficks with sun and weather;
Then lifts an Indian paintbrush to the sky,
Half flame, half feather.

In desert places it is quite the same;
He delves at petal-plans, divinely, surely,
Until a bud too shy to have a name
Blossoms demurely.

He dares to sow the waste, to plow the rock.
Though Eden knew His beauty and His power,
He could not plant in it a yucca stalk,
A cactus flower.

Jail Bird

I am a prisoner in a cell of trees;
Great walls of green
Close in about me; the attendant breeze
Fetches me fare
Of simple and sufficing air.
My pallet is the straight turf, hard and clean.
My leafy window bars
By day let in three slender beams of sun, by night three innocent stars.

It was the face
Of beauty brought me captive to this place
Where now I lie in indolent disgrace!

For who am I
To be in this wise made
Thrall to a sweet-faced glade,
I who am kin to mountain-top and cloud?
Why not deal cunningly, devise some tool
To freedom and escape from this adventureless school?
Why not break prison bonds and fly
Up, up to where
The high hills and the high heavens lie bare
With no tree nigh?
Beauty, outrivalled, may behold me there,
Aloof, austere, most inaccessible, most proud
To die,
A convict hooded in cerulean shroud
On mountain gallows by the hangman sky.

Now is my plot well laid!
Presently I shall pick these locks of shade,
Shall drug with morning mist the vigilant hours,
Shall dare the gauntlet of belaying flowers,
And, fugitive, shall run
Out to my mountain freedom and keen air,
Into the arms of the sun!

Commentary

A MOTHER TO HER CHILD

The pine tree in the snow cannot know joy;
But you are come to me, flower of strength and whiteness,
Bearing implicit fruit of love.

OPINION

If all the sky should quiver into pinions,
And all the air should tinkle into silver singing,
The earth would still have need, I think, for bluebirds.

THE CHERRY TREE

The world is filled with You!
From what besides Your beauty could I have fashioned flower-buds?
Tomorrow You shall have cherry-blossoms, my Maker.

Concerning Death

ENLIGHTENMENT

My moonlit night is a young girl, death-sick, pale,
With candles dimly burning at her bed. The dawn will come to fetch her.
Meanwhile I wait and watch, thinking to learn another lovely thing of
    death.

I ASK MY TEACHERS

Why do you wrap your wisdom in a multitude of words?
My master, Death, who will enlighten me completely and forever,
Employs no speech at all.

THE DAY NO LETTER COMES

The day you do not write and silence follows, to be broken only by my
    life's end,
I shall know that you have not forgotten, that now you love me perfectly,
For I shall understand that you are dead.

DEATH

The moon does not change.
Tonight a shadow shuts from me its borrowed beauty!
This will be divinely true of you when you are dead.

Personalities

VIRGINS

Though they be lovers, this lithe wind and his clean maid, the snow,
She has no thought to hold him, nor will he
Touch with his innocent importunities the whiteness of herself.

BECAUSE NO WORD IS IMPOSSIBLE WITH GOD

The ancient winter and the ancient earth
Have known each other; presently
There will be born to them that strange, alluring, predilect wonder-child,
    the spring.

PROTEST TO THE WIND

Though who shall set the bounds to your dominion,
Yet am not I your slave
That you should lash me with the whip of your keen fury.

TIRED CHILD

The petulant night has sobbed herself to sleep.
Demurely she will wake
In the serene forgetfulness of dawn.

Distinctions

I have thought life a sword by which I cleave existence, birth to death,
    in twain;
I have regarded life to be experience so sundered;
Now I know life to be the ultimate beyond my keen, irrevocable blade
Waiting your word, my lover.

Reported Sunset

Who believes our report of this still event
Of sunset in casual silver spent
On the world's west wall, of silver intent
In the lake's long line, of silver lent
To the air for luster and deep content:
Who believes our report of this still event?

Presentation

Two doves I bring;
One broods all day;
One has a broken wing;
One is the prayer I have no words to say;
One is the song I have no words to sing.

Motif for Mary's Dolors

Seven notes of grief,
Seven points of pain,
Scale struck to start
What melodies and
What refrain
Within your song-swept heart!

Candle-Light

Day has its sun,
And night the stars,
But God has candle-light.

Upon the world's great candle-stick He sets
The little taper of yourself ashine,
That when the sun has sputtered out
And all the stars are dead,
Your immortality may flame and burn
Across His infinite immensity forever.

Wherefore He will sometime blow out the sun,
And snuff the stars,
Preferring candle-light.

Communion

Having held you
I have held whiteness intense and austere as the snows that rest
On that far, lone mountain, against my breast.
I have held whiteness more shining and splendid than clouds that start
In still skies of summer, upon my heart.
I have held whiteness more wistful and dear than a child's alarms,
Than a flower upfolded, within my arms.
I have held whiteness that burns like a flame, that broods like a dove
In my soul forever,—I have held love.

Song

You are the young moon's bright
Joy in the innocent white
Snow, are the stars' delight
In their deep heaven's height.
Sweet, read my song aright.
You are my love. Good night.

Hyères

(From Sainte Claire le Château) *

This is no city lying at my feet.
It is, I think, some bravely blazoned shield,
Fair as the sun and by the sun annealed;
Its proud device of avenue and street
A hundred palms and platan trees repeat;
Vermilion roofs upon an azure field
Quartered with garden greens, and, wonder-keeled,
The ocean, argent, crescent, incomplete.

There are so many things that one forgets,
But never this sun-smitten shield of France
With, for its crest, rampant against the sky,
A single eucalyptus, greaved and high,
And, couchant at the heart of old romance,
Field upon field of breathing violets.

* The home of Edith Wharton.

99

Stonehenge

This may have been a temple to the sun,
This enigmatic pile of Druid stone.
Across its western portal may have shone
The springtime dawn that lighted Babylon.
Something like this the pharaohs might have done,
Imposing rock on rock, erect or prone,
Inert, bloodstained, wind-beaten, weather-blown,
In dogged protest to oblivion.

Not with such stolid ponderosity
Do I adore the light and love the sky.
Fluttering from tangled grasses at my feet
A skylark, fugitive and silver-sweet,
My worship is, or southward, lifted high,
The simple lyric spire of Salisbury.

Fragmentary—Your Garden

I have not ever seen your garden though
I well surmise the February wonder
By which your hyacinth and crocus sunder
Earth and themselves in patterns that they know.
I guess your tulip's flame, your jonquil's glow,
That dear half miracle, half velvet blunder
You call a pansy, and the golden plunder
The acacia shares with all the winds that blow.

But wherefore do I send this message? Pardon
My having thus much courage to begin it,
Who must not ever wander through your Arden
To pluck its rose or listen to its linnet,
Knowing how life has grown your braver garden
For love that has and has not blossomed in it.

Mid-Ocean

We know our mountains well, their winds, their weather.
Horizons high and white in the heavenly hush
Of sun or moonlit snow; the ecstatic rush
Of pentecostal spring in leaf and feather;
Wild altitudes of blossoming summer, whether
Cliff rose, pentstemon's blue, or lupine's flush;
Autumn's apocalyptic burning bush:
All these we have loved rapturously together.

Sometime, beloved, we shall see the ocean,
Not continents apart and separately;
Then all this passionate peace, this passionate motion,
Wonder, omnipotence, immensity,
We shall possess beyond all word, all notion,
Silent, together, looking out to sea.

Of What Avail

I will withstand my white love to her face,
My silver moon. O, bitterest thing to do!
I cannot be her thrall and lover, too.
I must have freedom for a little space
From her inevitable beauty, her still grace,
Her nonchalant way across the night's dim blue,
Her winds of mere caprice. Yes, I will sue
For respite and release, some temperate place

Of peace. But when these delicate bonds I sunder
What shall avail me my accomplished quest?
What wings of freedom can I hide me under,
Or whither flee when next she walks the west
In all her innocent tyranny of white wonder,
With twilight's simple blossom at her breast?

In the Face of Failure

I wonder shall I see spring come this year?
A score of Aprils I have asked the same,
Dreaming at last to learn the miracle game:
Winds woven of delight; skies intimate, near;
Small, inexperienced, perfect leaves; the dear
Young rain; a quick green devastating flame
Sweeping the world; then the ineffable name
Spoken with certainty;—so, spring is here.

And all my foresight leaves me unprepared!
Occultly bonds are broken, cerements tattered;
I only know by whom, for I have dared
To let myself be caught divinely, shattered
By spring. If ultimate secrets I had shared
I must have died. Then nothing else had mattered.

Return

This is your home to which you are returning.
Because you have so hungered for the place,
Shall we not stop to say the simple grace
That you have spent a passionate lifetime learning?
Upon the hearth a brave, new fire is burning;
The flowers you hoped would greet you in the vase
You wished, are here; here that grave, tender face
You tell me is the sum of all your yearning.

The threshold's peace, impatient to possess you,
More lovely than, homesick, you clamored for;
Music at once to shatter and caress you;
The voice you dream, the hands that you adore;
All, all are here to welcome and to bless you.
Come to my waiting heart! What will you more?

California Spring

Such spring as one has need of here is ended,
With signs scarce marked and mercifully few:
Leaves for the eucalyptus, white and new;
The threadbare hills with great, green patches mended,
But not as if a new world were intended.
What need? And so I watch the noon's high blue
And dare, with April here, to think of you.
Suppose the acacia were more subtly splendid!

Suppose such life, such beauty, hour by hour
Came creeping on me, stealthily, like a thief!
What weapon have I for a gradual flower
Or what defense against a folded leaf;
To parry long, sure thoughts of you what power?
Yes, spring has shown me mercy, being brief.

Details for My Burial

As for the matter of my burial,
It follows hard the golden day I die.
There needs but a small grave where I may lie,
Cut in the snow's white peace I love so well,
Or sweetened with young rain,—one cannot tell—
But always, always the great, solicitous sky,
The quick, close earth, and all that live thereby.
Dear God, how I desire the consecrate cell!

It holds divine reprieves, immortal pardons
Whereby my vagabond feet are stricken free;
My fingers busy here with mortal gardens
May plant and pluck to ultimate ecstasy.
Myself? A heavenly tramp in heavenly Ardens!
Remember, when you dig a grave for me.

AMERICAN TWELFTH NIGHT

David

Speak, young boy of God;
When blossoms the predilect flower of Jesse's quick rod?
Out of Saba when come those grave kings by a light
Newborn to the night?

The mountains of Juda, when leap they with laughter and mirth
At a Bethlehem birth?
Speak, David, child-seer of star and of sky;
The time, is it nigh?

A flower of Jesse, a shepherd you are,
A king and a star,
A song to the glory of God, and a singer who thrills
All the Judean hills.
These signs, are they met and embraced and come true,
Or frustrate in you?

Nay, the root and the rod and the bud have their use and their hour,
But Christ is the Flower.
A shepherd but not to be led to the slaughter am I,
To bleed and to die;

A king who the robe of a fool and the thorn crown has known
In vision alone;
A singer whose heart must cry out through the joy of his song,
"How long, Lord,—how long?"
A watcher who looks through the mist over Bethlehem's hills for a thou-
    sand slow years,—
A mist that is tears.

Dialogue

A Word, a Word
Thou, Lord, didst utter which Thy willing handmaid heard,
And infinite, small Life within my own life breathed and stirred.

A blessed space
My Lord in me and I in Him found resting place;
In such divine repose I waited, silent and full of grace.

Answer is nigh;
O God, I lift a Child up heart-and-heaven high
And say, "This is my Flesh and Blood"; Thy Word is my reply.

Swaddling Clothes

My days are all white with wonder, the wonder of stitching and sewing,
Making a spotless garment for Mary's spotless Son;
My hours are bright with joy as I watch the small robe growing,
The little robe of love that will compass the infinite One.

Love is the cloth it is made from; my heart possesses no other;
Love is the pattern, too, that I trace with unfaltering care;
Love is my double thread; the love of the Son and the mother;
Woven throughout of love, think you it will be fair?

Aye, and the mother Mary will let her little One wear it,—
He Who has never in aught save divinity been arrayed,—
All upon Christmas morning; O heart of me, can you bear it,
The joy of your God appareled in raiment your love has made!

Possession

I cannot chant the angels' hymn
As did the hosts of seraphim.

I cannot even cross the wild
As shepherds did, to find the Child.

I cannot shine, a living star,
To guide grave magi from afar.

I have no incense, myrrh, or gold
For gift as had the kings of old.

In all the world there is nowhere
A place so poor, a spot so bare

Save the rude cave at Bethlehem town
Where Christ, my Savior, laid Him down.

Because I am like that mean stall
I may possess Him most of all.

Ways

God has most simple ways.
He likes a stable's covering,
And little lambs that shepherds bring.
His majesty aside He lays,
You would not know He is a King,
He has such humble ways.

See, where He lies, quite sweet and small,
A Baby in an ox's stall
Smiling to meet His mother's gaze.
You could not fear this God at all,
He has such tender ways.

But look you, how the heavens blaze!
And hark you, what angelic praise
Resounds! Indeed, He is a King,
And these be Godlike ways.

Stars

We are the stars that have watched the night skies with the prophets of
    old;
We are the magi from out of the East; we are bringers of gold.

Heaven has incense of praise from censers seraphic to bring;
Earth, the world-weary, bears bitter-sweet treasure of myrrh to the King.

Homage of incense and myrrh for a God and a Saviour are meet;
We are your stars, little King, and we scatter the gold of ourselves at Your
    feet.

A Word for Shepherds and Angels

I spoke to Gabriel and was not afraid;
But to these herdsmen, hardy keepers of sheep,
And their singing midnight skies, what reply shall be made?

I may say to them—it were a gracious thing to do—
"My Son when grown to a man, my Child asleep,
He will care for flocks; He will be a shepherd, too."

Then mayhap their hearts will be opened as mine, with pain;
They may understand how my first-born, my only One
Will be our unblemished Lamb—and slain, and slain!

Angels and shepherds and I have known, have heard
Tidings to shatter the earth and amaze the sun.
Angels and shepherds, tonight I bring you the Word.

American Twelfth Night

Three men have just arrived,
Wise men from the West,
The continent of Christopher Columbus,
The Christ-bearer, the Dove.
They have journeyed far;
They have travelled a bitter way,
Seeking You to adore You.

The gifts they offer are past price, past precedent.

One brings You a lost continent.
One brings You his ambiguous liberty.
One brings his wealth of hallowed and unhallowed gold.

Red, black, and white, they come to You as brothers.

Make them, O Christ, three in one after Your image!
Keep them, O God, one in three in Your own likeness.

Christmas: Elizabeth Watches the Night Sky

I think the clouds tonight
Are lambs and wayward sheep
Huddled and lost and white.
My boy stirs in his sleep!

At midnight he awoke
As at an uttered word.
I only guess who spoke
And what he heard.

His eyes, before he slept,
Grew deep as prophets' are.
Up from their darkness leapt
Light like a star.

Two clouds drift in the blue.
How strangely moved I am!
They are like a lone ewe
And her young lamb.

A Song of Bedlam Inn

My gate stands open,
My window alight;
I shall wait at the threshold
Through the still night.

And if my love comes
On tired feet,
I shall hear his footsteps
In the still street.

I shall lift the latch
Like a broken wing,
For he knows my life
Is a shattered thing.

I shall open the door
With a broken cry,
For the night that I let
My love pass by.

But I shall say
No word at all.
For the sound of his step,
For his low call

My gate stands open,
My window alight.
My love and your love
Will come tonight.

Christmas in Provence

I

MIDNIGHT MASS

Tonight this city seated on a hill
Wears its mediaeval fortress like a crown
Above a brow too peace-possessed to frown.
Its ancient church watches the darkness fill
With quiet aureoles of light that spill
Through little streets that clamber up the town.
Here ancient, royal kings have laid them down,
And here, this night, a King will rest Him still.

I had not known that night could be so holy;
I had not thought that peace could be so deep.
O passion of night and peace, possess me solely!
O passion of love, be mine this night to keep!
O little climbing streets, lead me up slowly
To where the King I wait for lies asleep!

THE SERENADE

This age-old church, dream-stricken yesterday,
Has wakened into loveliness and light
And all Provence is in its arms tonight,
And all its tambourines and fifes are gay.
The dull, encumbering ages fall away;
Templar and king kneel in the ancient rite
With torches' blaze and candles tall and white
And a Child cradled on the fresh-strewn hay.

Then the night fills with song, laughing and leaping,
This music of a thousand lyric years,
A serenade of love where love lies sleeping,
The minstrelsy of God where God appears,
And where I kneel, bemused, song-shaken, weeping,
A happy-hearted troubadour in tears.

Christmas Eve

I journeyed down to Bethlehem
In deep peace on a winter day.
I think a young girl and a man
Were with me on the way.

And in the little town at dusk
The young girl waited in the street.
The stones and I were very glad
With kissing of her feet.

A tender wind encompassed her;
The waiting world, the listening air,
The watching stars grew sweet and white
With kissing of her hair.

The earth was wise as any child
Because she was so young and wise,
And all the dark was luminous
With looking in her eyes.

Tonight I wait upon my knees
Beside her in this quiet place,
Loving the wonder in her heart,
The wonder in her face.

Bethlehem

On Christmas eve in Bethlehem town
The shadows fall; the night comes down;
The stars shine clear; the winds grow mild;
An inn stands open for a Child
On Christmas eve in Bethlehem town.

In Bethlehem on Christmas day
One manger is fresh strewn with hay,
And you will find a young Child there,
And you will find a lady fair
In Bethlehem on Christmas day.

All roads must lead to Bethlehem;
All men at last must follow them;
And be you great or be you small
The sweet Lord Jesus bless you all
Upon the roads to Bethlehem.

Christmas Night 1940

There is a night too circumspect for stars,
A night too still and suppliant for song.
Kings do not walk abroad nor shepherds watch.
None save a Child is strong.

This night has fallen; more desired than dawn
The splendor of a Child will wake the skies.
Peace will be in His heart and on His lips,
And pity in His eyes.

Voices are crying through the wilderness
And children wander in a nameless land.
This night a Child is born. Some know His name
And some may understand.

New Things and Old

Christmas 1941

The dark is shattered
With wild, new fear;
An ass's feet stumbling
Is the sound that I hear.

The night is brighter
Than the day should be;
A strange star's splendor
Is the light that I see.

And above the terror
Of earth and sky
I can hear, if I listen,
A young Child's cry;

I can see, if I look,
Legions of wings,
And a woman who ponders
On all these things.

Sheepfolds

The shepherds are stricken; the sheep have fled;
Their folds are broken, their watch-fires dead.

Not only the lost and wayward one;
The ninety-nine, they, too, are undone.

The laden ewes, the driven sheep,
Where can they lay their young to sleep?

This Lamb, new-born and weak and cold,
This Lamb of God,—will you be His fold?

To Be Enrolled

This is the month for census-taking.
I come to be enrolled in Bethlehem,
The House of Bread, to which I legally belong.

Already I foresee that not one of its hostels will receive me.
I shall seek lodging in a manger-cave at the town's edge.
Joseph, my kinsman, will be there
With Mary, his espoused wife, and her Child
Who is the Son of God.

This year and every year He comes to Bethlehem
To be enrolled among the sons of men.
And I, who am the merest of them,
I also am a son of God.
I also come to be enrolled with Him.

Christmas

This is the hour to which all hours lead.
The table is spread with fine white linen.
Bread and wine and water are set out.
A great book stands ready from which the prayers and
    history of this day will be read.
We are to eat by candlelight.
The tapers are already burning.
This is a feast of love.
Christ is our host.
You and I are to be His guests.
This is Christ's Mass.
It is the hour to which all hours lead.

The Light

You do not know, you cannot, cannot guess
Across what burning sands I come to you;
Over what difficult seas, upon what new
Hard ways of exile, ways of loneliness.

You did not think of gifts—my piteous three;
Worthy I thought them—kings had such of old.
Do you keep but the frankincense and gold,
And leave the bitterness of myrrh to me.

Bid me, I will return into the night.
Remember only, you who merciful are,
I found you by the shining of a star,
So I must walk forever in its light.

Christmas Song

The earth is very beautiful with stars
And there are wise men yet who love their light,
Shepherds who watch their flocks and gather songs
From the still night.

And though the hostels of the world be thronged,
Its mangers wait, its stable doors swing wide.
Mary, young girl, this is their hour and yours;
Come, come inside!

Jesus, young child, content You here to lie
Among clean kine and men bemused with awe.
Remember, dearling, when You made Your world
You willed this straw.

The world is blind; the world is Bethlehem
But over it Your stars are very bright.
With weak and wise, with Mary here I am,
Young child, tonight.

Ballad of the Happy Christmas Wind

I am a happy Christmas wind;
I am courteous; I am kind.

I walked the way to Bethlehem town
Beside our Lady going down.

I know the inn she stood before;
I would have beaten down the door;

I thought on Mary and the Child;
I blew gently; I grew mild.

I ran ahead to find a house
To shelter Mary and her spouse.

I found a stable, loosed the door,
The cave they had been seeking for.

Because they had a place to bide
I was so glad, alone outside,

I ran across the hills for joy!
I waked a little shepherd boy,

And all the older shepherds stirred
At what they felt and what they heard

124

Of angel music, heavenly things!
I caught the song and gave it wings.

I ran across the midnight blue;
I ran across the ages, too;
I have it, have it here for you.

A Child is born for you again;
A Son is given, is given to men!
I am a singing wind. Amen.

A Nun Speaks to Mary

I

IN THE DAYS OF KING HEROD

You had no little maid, so I remember,
To help you sweep and tidy up the room,
To sit and watch with you that first December
Through shining twilights deep with golden gloom.

Through all those wistful days you had no mother
To know your wonder and to share your joy
Of fashioning—you could not let another!—
The darling swaddling garments for your Boy.

There was not any housewife to befriend you
The day word came to go to Bethlehem town;
No kinswoman bethought her to attend you
Of all the folk of David going down.

And when you held Him to your heart in wonder,
Emmanuel, God's Son, your Boy, the Word
Made flesh Who shook the skies with holy thunder,
In Bethlehem not any mother stirred.

II

SEQUEL

Now come again the sweet Isaian days,
Merciful, tender;
I know their loneliness; I dream their splendor.
Down their plain ways,
Mary, I come,
Confounded with this former shame, and dumb.
Take me in service, in complete surrender,
Walking and sleeping;
Take every daily task, take every duty,
Take little homely things as dusting, sweeping;
Change them into your heavenly housekeeping;
Touch them with Nazareth's most stricken beauty.
Think that my busy hands weave raiment fair
For Christ to wear;
Know that my hurrying feet
Run all your errands, Sweet;
And should they tarry,
Hear how I promise them,

My Lady Mary,
That they at length may go with you to Bethlehem.
And at the last let be
On those three mute and piteous, fearful days
When none of all earth's womenfolk is near you,
That you will have to help you and to cheer you
In little foolish ways
Poor, simple me;
That when you stand outside the inn, the night wind blowing,
I will be there
Adoring, knowing;
That if the whole wide world should have no room,
I will be waiting through whatever gloom
To be your resting place.—But this is heaven I dare!

So, let my promise be my prayer.
And do not seek for any cave at all
With patient kine and manger crib and stall
Beyond the gates of little Bethlehem town
To lay your dear Son down.
Mother, all fair,
Lay Him within my hungry arms to sleep;
Lay Him within my hungry heart to keep,
Adorable, holy,
Little and lowly.
And let earth's shepherds, let heaven's seraphim
So find me with you Christmas night, adoring, loving Him.

At Shadow Time

I watch the shadow folk creep down,
The white-faced stars climb up the sky;
I hear the little winds go by;
I see the far lights of the town.

I feel that peace is over them
And out of it this word I hear,
"The blessed time is very near,
The holy night at Bethlehem."

Over and over I repeat,
"O Bethlehem, O holy night,
O angel host, O starry light
Above a Baby small and sweet."

Then how I wish that I had been
A holy king, a shepherd dumb;
With what glad haste I would have come
To see the things that they have seen!

Scarce do I wish when lo! I see
A Lady in God's beauty dressed,
A sleeping Babe upon her breast,
Walk past me very quietly.

I think she comes a far, far way;
I think she walks the wide world's gloom,
Seeking somewhere a little room
In which her precious Child to lay.

But now her eyes grow large and bright;
I see that she has found a place,
And from the smile upon her face
The darkness blossoms into light.

"Here is a place, my little One,"
She whispers low, "where You may bide;
And room there is for me, beside;
A place of love it is, my Son.

"A place kept but for You alone;
And look You, what a beauteous thing,
Here You will reign, my little King,
Where love has built for You a throne."

Gently she lays her Babe to rest
In this place holy and apart;
The place I know; it is your heart
That loves this Child and loves Him best.

Then once again do I repeat,
"O Bethlehem, O holy night,
O angel host, O starry light
Above a Baby small and sweet."

I watch the shadows fall and hear
The little winds; I take your hand
In mine and we both understand
That Bethlehem is very near.

Wishes

The Christmas stars at Bethlehem
Shone very clear and bright;
Oh, may they shine with light divine
For you this Christmas night!

The Christmas winds at Bethlehem
Folded their wings away;
May every wind blow gently kind
For you on Christmas day.

The angel hosts at Bethlehem
Sang "Peace on earth to men";
And may their song ring loud and long
Within your heart again.

The shepherds come to Bethlehem
Knelt in rapt wondering;
To Bethlehem, oh, haste with them
To see the little King!

The holy pair at Bethlehem
Looked upon them and smiled;
Would it might be your lot to see
These blest ones and the Child.

The little Babe at Bethlehem
Gave them His hand to kiss;
And oh, I pray your heart today
May know such joy as this.

Parables

Because we are all innkeepers, tonight
Let every door be open, every window bright,
That, when a young girl and her waiting Child shall come,
We be their home.

Because we are all shepherds on the hills,
Keeping whatever be our flocks, when the night fills
With songs to say a Child is born in Bethlehem,
We follow them.

Because we are as wise as wise men are,
We find in every star a wild, prophetic star.
Tonight we seek, way-worn, life-laden, one star's light
Out of our night.

Christmas Trees

Gift-laden all
great trees and small;

these, surely, these
are Christ's, Christ's trees.

Spring's pregnant hour
bears leaf, bears flower,

Which He transmutes
to summer fruits.

October's flame
burns with His name.

Fir trees and spruce
await His use.

High on its hill
one lone tree will

its great boughs lift
with Christ for gift.

God-laden all,
great trees and small,

green trees and gray
on Christmas day
give Christ away.

Christmas Itinerary for Any Priest

I am a wayfarer,
A traveller with holy oils upon his hands,
Journeying from Nazareth to Bethlehem,
Journeying from God to God.

Pilgrims from all the world, a multitude, are with me.
You are among them, you and you.

A girl is with us on the way.
Rather, to tell the golden truth, she is the way.
We speak together only in the silence of the Word beneath her heart.

We pass the wide inn of the world
Knowing it has not room enough to house the Guest she bears.

Now night has fallen
And we have come to Bethlehem.

At midnight we shall find her in a stable,
Among the gentle beasts of earth
And simple folk, as shepherds are,
And millions upon millions of her angels.

She will be holding close her new-born, only Son, the Son of God,
Saying within her wondering heart, "This is my body, this my blood."
And she will lift Him up for us to see and to adore.

Presently I, the wayfarer, with holy oils upon his hands,
Shall say her selfsame words, "This is My Body, this My Blood,"
Holding the Son of Mary, holding God.

★
O
HOLY
WOOD
OF CRIB
AND ROOD
TODAY LET BE
Y
O
U
R
CHRISTMAS TREE

FOUR GIRLS

Four Girls

It was the fourth of August, 1841. Four French girls knelt in the chapel of the Good Shepherd nuns in the town of Le Mans, France. Father Basil Moreau, a young canon from the cathedral, came into the sanctuary. A simple ceremony followed. The girls were clothed in plain serge habits and delaine veils. A new religious congregation had come into existence, the Marianites, Sisters of the Holy Cross.

> Le Mans was not concerned that August day,
> The vigil of Our Lady of the Snow;
> He was a dreamer, Basil Marie Moreau;
> You were four girls and young; one could not say
> That splendor in your folded futures lay.
> Kneeling at Mass a hundred years ago,
> Novices newly clad, you did not know
> How girlhood, France, and God possessed your way;
>
> How they possess it still, down all these years,
> And how new ways out of the old have led.
> Girls out of other worlds and other climes
> Have put on blessed black ten thousand times,
> Dreaming your dream, saying the prayers you said
> A hundred years ago, my dears, my dears!

Gates

The oranges at Jaffa gate
Are heaped in hills; men sell and buy
Or sit and watch the twisted road
Or David's tower against the sky.

The Golden Gate is walled with stone.
No king can pass nor prophet see
The valley of Jehosaphat,
The olives of Gethsemane.

St. Stephen's is a quiet gate,
A simple door that lets in dawn.
Its hill, its walls, its ancient stones,
What strange things they have looked upon!

Asses, belabored, stumble past;
Traffickers clamor; priests debate;
A child begs alms; a blind man gropes
To sunshine at Damascus gate.

The world has narrow gates and wide;
Men seek their loves through all of them
And I have come here, seeking mine,
Jerusalem, Jerusalem!

The Shopper

I knew the hills of Nazareth
Had miracles to tell.
I hoped the shops of Nazareth
Had memories to sell.
I climbed the streets of Nazareth
And bought a camel's bell.

At Cana's well in Galilee
One draws no wine today
And wedding guests in Galilee
Have no great word to say.
A beggar child in Galilee
Sold me a pot of clay.

In cobble-stoned Jerusalem
For hours and hours I stood.
I brought back from Jerusalem
The simplest thing I could,
A donkey from Jerusalem
Cut out of olive wood.

A house of bread is Bethlehem
And though I came from far
I did not shop in Bethlehem
Except to buy a bar
Of sunset over Bethlehem
And the first evening star.

From Mount Carmel

I will bring you this wind on the rock, as wild as a wind can be,
And, a thousand feet below, the tattered toss of the sea.

I will bring you the shadowy shapes of olive trees in the night,
The moon through a sudden rift of great clouds, huddled and white.

I will fill my arms with the wonder of stars in the midnight blue;
I will fill my eyes with the light of their shining to give to you.

I will bring you the rain-washed dawn in the cave of the prophet's rest,
And the little, sunlit cloud, like a man's hand, in the west.

Gather and count them all; tell me the single thing
You would have from Carmel's height is the gift that I cannot bring.

A hundred boys keep vigil of love at the prophet's cave.
They have bartered the world for Carmel; they are buying the gift you
crave.

Suez Canal at Sunset

Two long, low, level banks of sand and a long, low sky;
On a strong, straight leash of water a thoroughbred boat goes by.
Far to the south a single cluster of palm trees lifts itself like a cry.
Across the long, low, shifting levels and hills of sand comes no reply.
The light in the west that was gold and rose is dead now. I watched it
die.

Things To Be Loved

The Carceri, soft rain in February,
These two stone oaks, this sky of Giotto's blue,
Beds of hepatica and fritillary
In this square garden plot that Francis knew:

These things are to be loved. I know. I love them
In their still world, uplifted from the plain.
I choose for you the diffident dearest of them,
White fritillaries in the Umbrian rain.

Survivors on the French Riviera

The aloe can have died of blossoming
A hundred times and more
Since dream-and-travel-dazed Odysseus
Wandered this shore.

The punctual cypress can have sought the sun
Through seed and faultless spire
A hundred times since one has watched beside
A Roman fire.

A thousand years ago these low Alps knew
The dark moods of the Moor.
Of crescent, empire, or of Ithaca
Who can be sure?

There have survived these low Alps and the sky,
Mistral and ocean swell,
I and this delicately blossoming field
Of asphodel.

Cherwell River, Oxford

I am a silken highway none walks upon
Only, in beauty going, you, white swan,
Through the clear dawn.

I am a sleeping mirror, unconscious till
You lean above my face to gaze your grave eyes' fill
In me, silver-still.

I am a dreaming fountain, limpid, cold,
Sealed, save to you. Come, beauteous, bold,
To me to hold.

Beech Trees

I passed a wood of beech trees yesterday
And I am shaken with its beauty yet.
Why should my breath catch and my eyes be wet
Because a hundred trees some yards away
Know simply how to dress in simple gray,
Are poised beyond the need of epithet,
And beautiful past power to forget?
I dare not think how they will look in May.

They wore illustrious yellow in the fall.
Their beauty is no thing at which they guess.
And when they put on green, and when they carry
Fans open in the sun or folded small,
I'll look through tears at ultimate loveliness;
Beeches in May, beeches in February.

Old Soldiers

Look at this avenue. Do you not love it,
This regiment of trees in ranks of fours
Marching abreast, maples and sycamores?
It is a body-guard a king could covet.
I like its strength, but most, the beauty of it,
And this one thing too mere for metaphors,
Its gray-black-white with winter out-of-doors,
And any winter sky at all above it.

There is one austere veteran; you must know him,
That grave, gaunt sycamore, battered and white
And standing stark beneath the blue of noon.
What a fine debt of dignity we owe him!
But wait until you watch him through the night;
Wait till you see him sharp against the moon.

Of Mary

HONEY

Mary is the flower-field where
Bernard, the bee,
Drinks wild nectar to
Ecstasy.

FIRE

Dominic, the dog, his
Mouth aflame,
Is a firebrand lighted at
Mary's name.

DUMB OXEN

Mary, pray for Paris
And Bethlehem;
A dumb ox served you
In both of them.

PASSOVER NIGHT; MARY SPEAKS

Once I bought my Son back with
Pigeons white.
O Judas, have we no
Doves tonight?

Food for Sailors

Odysseus ate the lotus with his crew,
Forgot their home and thought that they were swine.
Who taste the flower of Jesse's blossoming rod
Remember Eden, know they are divine.

Speaking of Honest Men

Blow out your foolish lamp; here are two honest men,
Diogenes;
A thief and a blasphemer, or, I think, a God,
On gallows-trees.

A Child Asleep

This is the child you trusted to my keeping,
Remote, mysterious as all shy things are.
Against her heart the summer night is sleeping,
Against her lips the stillness of a star.

Limitations

Words I can pattern
Row after row.
How to plan a snowflake
I do not know.

I can fashion raiment
For me, for you,
But to clothe a pansy
What can I do?

I can plant a garden,
Set its paths with care.
Who will tell a dawn wind
To wander there?

I can fly forever
Where my love may be
And no bird, no thought can
Follow me!

Love and the Law

Your word is law. You lift these high horizons
Of mountains; stretch this long line of the sea;
Set me enamored and elate between them;
Then, with a breath, you take them all from me.

Your word is still my law. I vow to follow
What path you point, whatever trail you show.
Take when you will these blue stars of December,
This strange and silent loveliness of snow.

No, I retract; I will not sell the ocean,
My mountains and the blossoming stars above,
Peace and the snow and all my wild, white freedom
Except you swear by God your word is love.

At Winter's End

Buds are backward and winter lingers
But you, the eager, the quick, the wary,
Have found the first gold fritillary,
The clustered, rose-pink lady-fingers.

You have found, too, with cautious hunting,
That tricky one, the elusive towhee,
The tanager, splendidly shy and showy,
The summer-minded lazuli bunting.

I come not back with April weather;
Winds cannot woo nor sun unbind me.
Much as you seek, you cannot find me;
We shall not have this spring together.

But we warm our hearts at no dying ember.
Who can tell us how love is parted?
We are forever happy-hearted,
Having one springtime to remember.

October Birthday

Were I immortal only I would proffer
Tokens tremendous as a god can give:
Planets in leash, an earth whereon to live
With all October's fugitive gold in coffer,
Its moon a sorceress, its wind a scoffer,
Oceans it carries in a sandy sieve,
And stars aloof and undemonstrative.
Gifts casually infinite I could offer.

But as a woman and your love I bring you
The simple, homely things a woman must:
A little, human-hearted song to sing you,
My arms to comfort and my lips to trust,
The tangled moods that, autumn-wise, I fling you,
The frail and faulty tenderness of dust.

Meditation on Atlas

Atlas held the firmament
But could not see the sun;
He had the world between his hands
But did not have its fun.

He ate the bread of bitterness
Nor knew that bread is sweet;
Nor guessed the joy of outstretched arms,
The gayety of feet.

The earth was on his shoulders;
The sky was on the earth;
He did not know its wonder;
He did not know its mirth.

He knelt for aeons, burdened
With the whole unwieldy scheme
And he missed the point entirely
Of the grand, deific theme.

I have hung for years together
On a stark, two-branching tree.
It holds the earth and sky apart;
It binds them endlessly.

My tree becomes a table;
I have tasted of its food;
I have eaten of God's body;
I have dared to drink God's blood.

I am stretched out and uplifted
Among stars and planets piled
In the anguish of the prophets
And the weakness of a child.

I can hold the earth for Atlas
And the skies above his head;
I can hold the God Who made them
And He will not strike me dead.

Be strong and glad as God is;
Open your great arms wide
And set your feet against God's feet,
Atlas. Be crucified.

From an Afternoon Caller

I called at your
New house today
To hear the words
You do not say;

To watch the eyes
I cannot see,
The hands you do not
Give to me.

I waited there
A quiet while
In the lost wonder
Of your smile,

And found a home
Austere and new
That has enshrined
And hallowed you.

I love this house
Where you are dead.
Your new grave leaves me
Comforted.

Fare Well

Fare infinitely well,
You who have valorously dared
This last, unshared,
Unending and all-perfect quest;
You who at length can tell
The things God has prepared
Are best,
Are best.

Michaelmastide

Once there was England in September:
Michaelmas daisies by the wall,
Luminous beech trees to remember,
And the rooks' call.

Once there were mountains, maples turning.
Mute with this beauty that we knew,
Tangible, tender beyond all yearning,
Once there was you.

November Afternoons

Now they have come, these afternoons in November,
When all the air is still and branches are bare,
And the long, lovely light that I remember
Invades with luminous peace the untroubled air.

Off to the west a dozen trees together
Stand in gray loveliness, bemused with light;
Slender and silver they stand in the autumn weather,
Waiting the inevitable winter, the inevitable night.

Blossoming light they bear as a single flower,
And silence more singing-sweet than a lone bird's call.
Off to the west I stand, sharing their hour,
At peace with beauty and needing no song at all.

Sentries at Umbrian Farms

Poplars patrol the hills of Umbria
And sentinel cypress trees.
I think of Francis and young Anthony
Walking among these.

Here in my land are other Umbrian hills
And other Umbrian farms,
Holding a world to Francis dedicate
Safe in their copious arms.

Upon this hilltop, neighbor to the stars,
I guard his world and mine,
Watching with Brother Sun and Sister Moon
And this belovèd pine.

Snow Storm

The air is white and winds are crying.
I think of swans in Galway flying.

Winds are wings; snow is a rover;
Swans of Galway are flying over.

Winds are birds; snow is a feather;
Wild white swans are wind and weather.

Wings drift downward; snow is falling;
Swans are wild winds crying, calling.

Winds are white with snow but alway
Mine are white with swans from Galway.

Swords

I saw a man in Cairo
Swallow a naked sword.
The strangers there were startled;
The idlers there were bored.
A few threw him piasters
And pennies for reward.

I saw a girl in Salem
With brave and perfect art
Let seven swords of anguish
Be driven in her heart.
No stranger heard her murmur.
No idler saw her start.

The mountebank in Cairo
Still plies his braggart trade.
But all my soul is riven
With a sword that is a blade
And all my store of silver
Is given to the maid.

Dreams of the Rood

FERRY MAN

Christopher is Christ's ferry man
Across the flood.
I stand with arms outstretched and wide
And am Christ's rood.

HUNTER'S LICENSE

Midway above your antlered head,
Beautiful buck, Christ's cross is set.
There Eustace saw it shining once
And I can see it yet.

PARAPHRASE FROM THE "NUN'S RULE"

By quaint ways men keep things in thought.
Our sweet Lord Christ, to mind Him of us,
Wears piercing marks in hands and feet,
The more to love us.

The Thirteenth Station

There was a song of peace through all the air
The night that You were born.
How could I think of peace, my only Fair,
With that wild rapture torn?

Today the earth and sky are mute with woe
And every lip is dumb.
Holding You to my heart again I know
Peace and its price have come.

Petals and Wings

I have considered flowers of the field
And how they dwell
Silent, at peace, and beautiful,
Each in a wind-walled cell.

And I have thought on wild, unlettered birds,
Song-silver things,
Free on their little leash of air;
I have considered wings.

I have dreamed petalled peace, and wilding flight
Into the sun.
Whose is the ultimate blossoming?
Whose the empyrean?

I know the Maker of all birds, all flowers.
He understands
The bud that breaks, the bird that flies
To freedom in His hands.

Song for a Nun's Cell

My love has made a room for me
That looks upon eternity.

Of His arm's length is every wall,
Infinitely large and small.

And He has set in it a bed;
At night I dream my love is dead.

A candle burns against the night;
Love is my darkness, love my light.

There is a table, small and fit;
Love breaks my bread and blesses it;

And for my rest a little stool;
Once men enthroned my love a fool.

Mayhap a fool bides in my cell.
Ah! who can tell, and Who can tell?

Wardrobe

My love gave me a king's robe,
Mock purple and red;
My love gave me a white coat,
A fool's coat, He said;
My love gave me a weft crown
Of thorns for my head.
Because He is my true love
He wore them instead.

Peace by Night

A velvet beautiful and dark
With hunched horizon lines of trees,
A silence boundaried by stars:
I will remember these;

And all our speech resolved into
An utter impotence of words,
Helplessly mute with living song
Like dream-bewildered birds.

Beyond this time of breathing peace,
This moth-still mystery of night,
I shall not need the dawn's elate
Apocalypse of light.

Leave me this hour of deep content
With darkness upon darkness spread,
Your face against its velvet set,
And blue stars overhead.

Statement

Nothing caught fire from the moon
Smouldering on the east horizon.
Three gaunt boughs of the sycamore
Were charred by night against it
And the banked embers of its splendor
Burn in my memory yet.

Easter Chronicle

Today is Easter; I am at Solesmes.
The air is still and delicate and sweet.
Violets cloud the path before my feet
And edge the village with their purple hem.
Alone, bemused with song, I gather them,
Thinking how, on this morning, I should meet
Blossoming sound, antiphonal, complete,
Blossoming color, leaf and flower and stem.

It has unfolded for me like a flower,
This great Gregorian chant: the solemn Mass,
The morning Office, hour by heavenly hour.
There shall remain, when lesser praise shall pass,
This music that is peace and prayer and power,
These April violets in the quickened grass.

Design

I am a young tree.
I have not ever made a flower.
My almond blossoms?
I am not too perplexed
How to devise them,
For I have learned by heart
The patterns of the morning sky.

Recital

No, you cannot touch it;
No, you cannot see
The beauty that I wear tonight
Delicately.

Oh! but you can hear it;
Oh! but you can know
How clad in song for your delight
Deftly I go.

Prayer Before Music

O Holy Spirit, come;
Rest on these inarticulate hands and dumb!

Be fire
For my elate desire.

Be wind
To quicken the still music of my mind.

Be the heard
Utter, ineffable word.

Teach, Holy One, with Your love's art
My hands, my heart.

Yours be the tongue
In which the songs of my desire are sung.

Lady Day Recital

They are a vase, these my two hands,
Delicate, deft and strong.
Lady, I bring them to you, blossom-filled
With flowers of song.

Music

I am a blind,
brave, captive, beautiful wind.

I am the bare,
dextrously patterned air.

I am mere sound
deliberately bound.

I am its key
to ecstatic liberty.

And I am speech
beyond words' lettered reach,

Vicarious lips
touched to apocalypse.

Wordless and bound and blind,
I bring peace to your heart and beauty to your mind.

162

To a Very Old Harness-Maker

(My Father)

Here are your harness shop, your world of leather,
Collars and hames and harness on the wall,
Summer-brown farmers come to town in fall,
Or stamping snowy boots in winter weather;
Here are your art of putting straps together,
Stitching-horse, needled wax-threads, accurate awl,
Your delicate ear, quick to the first bird's call,
Your delicate eye, quick to its moulted feather.

Here at your desk the day's accounts are ended,
Your world resolved upon, your gardens planned,
Your simple earnings totaled or expended,
Leather goods bought and sold, poetry scanned.
Here I remember you, smiling and quaintly splendid,
A gathered moss rose in your wax-brown hand.

Mirrors

I seek you always. Have I never seen you?
Let's ask if any bird has seen the air,
Or flower the light, though these are everywhere.
Choose any veil you will. Set it between you
And my beholding. Know it shall not screen you
From me. What occult vestures you may wear,
Too dread or dull or difficult to bear,
Are mirrors meaning naught unless they mean you.

Is beauty something I cannot discover?
Is truth a thing that only children know?
Are you not mine who are the whole world's lover?
Can I not find you in all winds that blow,
In the wild loneliness of lark and plover,
In slender shadow trees upon the snow?

Design for a Stream-Lined Sunrise

If you must draw mere beauty,
Subtend one third of the whole arc of heaven
With a gray chord of cloud
Stretched from the quick southeast to the still dubious west.
Edge all the chord with white, bright, mutable silver.
Draw it on cloudlessness at daybreak,
If you would draw mere beauty.

But you cannot do this
Because the artless air achieved this brief design for sunrise
Once and forever,
Today, at dawn,
And then this long line, cutting with sheer simplicity of silver
The breathless, deep-blue arc of the south,
Became, because of my beholding,
Beyond potential beauty, beautiful.

You Ask My Age

I am older than dawn
And sunset are.
I can think past the light
Of the oldest star.

The piled-up mountains
And ancient trees,
Timeless rivers
And ageless seas;

East and west winds,
South and north;
I know the hour
That brought them forth.

How old am I?
As days are told,
The earth is younger
Than I am old.

Years cannot measure
Time for me.
Fetch us the clock
Of infinity.

This is the answer
If you would know;
From life I come;
To life I go.

Wherefore I am
More gladly young
Than a child not born,
Than a song not sung;

More young than the spring
Before its birth,
Than the dreaming life
In the dreaming earth;

More young than the hosts
Of seraphim
Who sing, "Hosanna,
Elohim."

Older I am
Than any star
And younger than
The angels are.

My Best Dress

This dress I wear with absolute, heavenly grace.
A hundred gowns I've wished for, asked or hinted;
A hundred fabrics dreamed of, plain or printed.
But witcheries of linen, lawn and lace
Are mere accessories to these hands, this face,
This body whole, with naught amiss or stinted;
Made of a stuff of clay, divinely minted,
And textured through with life and time and place.

My mother wove it from her loveliness.
She wished it perfect; she assumed it brave.
Today, which is my life, I wear the dress
With all the pride and dignity she gave.
At night will some one take it, please, and bless
And put it neatly for her in my grave?

Hospitality

You ask me to your home,
You whom I love endlessly,
To stay
With you forever.
Let it be now.
Today
Is not too soon
To be with you forever!
You say
That death will come to fetch me.
Now?
Presently.
Let it be now.

To Mary

Dear Girl,—and if this hour
Must have farewell,
Then let it be in parable.
As through the sanctuary of your life one passed,
Into your white soul's treasury she cast
For dower
The substance of her living, all she had,
And giving her few small mites to you, was glad.

Dirge

The moon is dead,
That bright, seductive Mona Lisa daughter of the earth
Is dead.
The moon is dead.
And who, who, who,
And who will bury her?

Sputnik is here and Sputnik II, Yes, and Explorer.
But they are not grave-diggers.
At best they are but truant sons of earth
Bent on discovery.
Will they, one asks, even survive the wake?
Will they be present for the burial?

The funeral will be matter of cosmic concern.
One cannot guess how long the wake may last
Nor who of all the universe will come.

This much is sure;
Sputnik nor Sputnik II nor brave Explorer
Will live to follow to her grave the moon.

Who cares?
Earth still keeps vigil lights aglow about her,
Knowing how death can still be lovely and beloved.

And there will be no funeral.
We will not bury her, our wayward, own,
Our enigmatic, beautiful, dead sister.
We will not bury the moon.

Apology for Youth

Stand at my window;
watch them pass:
a lass and a lad,
a lad and a lass.

This is a way
to go to school,
learning an olden,
golden rule.

They seek for wisdom
in a book;
then they look up
and look—and look.

And wonder, wonder
if, after all,
wisdom is so
reciprocal.

They ask for beauty,
ask for truth
who have no thought
to ask for youth.

Theirs are the earth,
the sea, the sky;
they sing; they dance;
they float; they fly.

Why do they hurry,
hurry so?
Can they or will they
or do they know

They will earn some love;
they will learn some truth,
but never learn
nor earn back youth.

Stand at my window,
lad and lass;
let not this youth,
this young love pass.

Hold the wonder;
love the lore
you would one day change
the slow years for.

Of Dryads

Were I a dryad, as I well may be,
I would choose for my tree my true love's tree.

Genteel beeches in quiet gray,
These were fair homes in which to stay.

An oak tree house in fall, in spring,
What a burnished, tapestry-tasseled thing!

Redwoods, cedars, fir trees, all
I have considered, great and small.

Myrtle, olive, sycamore,
Palm, and many, many more.

But of earth's trees, this single one
I choose for dwelling beneath the sun.

I am a dryad; I live in a tree,
The tree that my true love wrought for me.

High on a hill this rood tree stands;
Its outstretched arms hold my outstretched hands.

The blood of its heart is my own heart's blood;
A dryad, I live in the holy rood.

Holy Communion in a Hospital

All of my life I have come to You, walking erect, hands clasped, head a
    little bowed;
Finding my way to You through the Sunday, the everyday crowd;
Kneeling to wait till You came to me in Your own inexplicable way,
Leaving me shaken with love and with less than nothing to say;
Always I came to You so; always until today.

Today You will come to me here in this room half-lighted, curtains a little
    drawn.
Never before have You sought me so, brought me Yourself at dawn.
Now You are helplessly here more than I, to feed me, to comfort, to bless;
Infinite, patient to bear with me pain's relentless caress;
Clothing me with Yourself, in the vesture of helplessness.

Ballade for the Queen of the World

It is not innocent organdy and lace;
It is not aureoles of lady-blue
That make illustrious haloes for your face
To crown the girl, the woman that is you.
Don any raiment of whatever hue;
Wear it with all the terrible grace you dare;
Make it an open secret. But the clue?
Who clothes you with the wonder that you wear?

Grant you a woman's everlasting grace;
Her mystery, once old, that now is new;
Grant in the world's wide, ever-changing place
Beauty that can be beautiful and true.
Queens have worn futile crowns in beauty's lieu.
Who set on you your shining crown of hair?
This regal thing only a King could do.
Who clothes you with the wonder that you wear?

You wore mortality a little space,
Lady of tears and laughter, myrrh and rue
Where seven swords of sorrow left sharp trace,
Whence seven joys their flaming splendor drew.
Bright as the sun from head to shining shoe,
Your majesty is here, is everywhere,
Too near to see, too palpable to view!
Who clothes you with the wonder that you wear?

Queen of the world, for servitude I sue,
Naming that name which is reply and prayer.
My hands in yours, I swear à Dieu, à Dieu
Who clothes you in the wonder that you wear.

Ballade on Eschatology

(For the Hero of the Habitually Relaxed Grasp)

Detachment is a virtue, teachers say.
Then let me practice it without regret.
What do I hold beyond this short today?
What cherish that I shall not soon forget?
These small things upon which my heart is set
Are matters for a heart's relinquishings.
One ultimate matter do I cleave to yet;
This, I shall not forget the four last things.

Remembrance, in a thief's unnoted way,
Filches from me with neither leave nor let
My thousand petty deities of clay.
Perhaps my eyes are still a little wet;
Perhaps my heart may still a little fret.
Detachment is the stuff of sunderings.
Time, so they tell me, is a brave asset.
And I shall not forget the four last things.

Your voice, your eyes,—or are they blue or gray?
The day we said good-bye, the day we met;
Hills we have walked, birds, flowers, our work, our play;—
Memory, how do you aid me and abet?
Time closes round me with impalpable net.
I'll not advert to clay or crowns or wings.
I have no thing to lose, all things to get,
For I shall not forget the four last things.

ENVOI

Lord, though by mortal tyrannies beset,
Immortal freedom in my wild heart sings.
A pauper comes to pay a pauper's debt.
God, I shall not forget the four last things.

Sister Madeleva has been one of the leading pioneers in the recent upsurge of genuine Catholic poetry that co cal insight with

Sister M. Madeleva is one of the outstanding women in the Catholic literary and academic fields. She has written over a dozen books of poetry and critical prose and has lectured to graduates and undergraduates, faculty members and students throughout the United States and Canada. Her work in the field of education, though concentrated in her duties as President of St. Mary's College for Catholic women, has encompassed national and international endeavors. Her recently published autobiography, *My First Seventy Years,* is a lively and entertaining book which fully reflects the accomplishments, charm and dignity of the author herself.

Her awards include the Sienna Medal, the National Poetry Center Award and, in 1948, recognition as the Catholic woman who has made a distinctive contribution to Catholic life in the United States. This year Sister Madeleva was awarded the Fifth Annual Campion Award by the Catholic Book Club for long-time and eminent service in the field of Catholic letters.